Richard III

Richard III
Fact and Fiction

Matt Lewis

PEN & SWORD HISTORY

AN IMPRINT OF PEN & SWORD BOOKS LTD.
YORKSHIRE – PHILADELPHIA

First published in Great Britain in 2019 by
Pen and Sword History
An imprint of
Pen & Sword Books Ltd
Yorkshire - Philadelphia

ISBN: 9781526727978

A CIP catalogue record for this book is available from the British Library.

Typeset in India By IMPEC e Solutions

Printed and bound in Great Britain by TJ International Ltd, Padstow, Cornwall

Pen & Sword Books Ltd incorporates the Imprints of Pen & Sword Books
Archaeology, Atlas, Aviation, Battleground, Discovery, Family History, History,
Maritime, Military, Naval, Politics, Railways, Select, Transport, True Crime,
Fiction, Frontline Books, Leo Cooper, Praetorian Press, Seaforth Publishing,
Wharncliffe and White Owl.

For a complete list of Pen & Sword titles please contact

PEN & SWORD BOOKS LIMITED
47 Church Street, Barnsley, South Yorkshire, S70 2AS, England
E-mail: enquiries@pen-and-sword.co.uk
Website: www.pen-and-sword.co.uk

or

PEN AND SWORD BOOKS
1950 Lawrence Rd, Havertown, PA 19083, USA
E-mail: Uspen-and-sword@casematepublishers.com
Website: www.penandswordbooks.com

Contents

Introduction

Few figures throw a larger or darker shadow over English and British history than King Richard III. To many, he remains a menacing figure, the irredeemably wicked uncle of fairy tales told to frighten children. For others, he is a wronged paragon of chivalry, a man maligned by those who defeated him and usurped his throne; the Tudors. Those less interested might be aware of a legend on the periphery of their knowledge, most often informed by William Shakespeare's masterpiece *The Tragedy of King Richard the Third*.

The debate around Richard III and his reputation burns hotter today than ever before. The discovery and reinternment of his mortal remains and the continued growth of social media have created fresh interest and provided a platform for the entrenchment of both views of Richard III. A virtual Wars of the Roses can now be played out all over again, driven by unshakeable convictions that can seem daunting and hard to understand to the more casual observer. Contradictory facts are launched from either side causing the deafening cacophony of explosive opinions that can make the real facts hard to discern and deter some from becoming embroiled in the debate.

Why is a man who was killed in battle over 500 years ago still attracting such passionate debate? How does a medieval king who reigned for only just over two years have a thriving fan club in the Richard III Society? Part of the reason lies in the mythologising of the facts about him, so many of which are open to the broadest interpretation so that both sides will claim them to make polar opposite points. The purpose of this book is to try and peel away some of the myths to reveal the bare, unadorned facts. Did Richard III invent bail? Did he murder a Lancastrian Prince of Wales, a king, his brother and his two nephews? Did he mean to marry his niece? Why did those previously loyal to the House of York abandon Richard III for an obscure Welshman in exile?

These questions and more will be answered as the facts are carefully dissected from the myths to reveal a man who should never be viewed as saint or sinner. Richard was a real man, who grew up, lived through, was affected by, and in turn influenced, hard times, when a country was at war with itself. The Wars of the Roses is itself a misleading term cast across decades of civil unrest and dynastic changes. In the early 1450's, Richard's father, Richard, Duke of York fell into opposition to his Lancastrian cousin, King Henry VI. When Henry fell seriously ill in 1453, it was to York that the government turned to act as Protector until the king's recovery at Christmas 1454. At the First Battle of St Albans in 1455, York did not try to take Henry's crown but instead fought Edmund Beaufort, Duke of Somerset for the right to act as Henry's chief advisor. The king attempted to reconcile the two factions at his court but could not control the disputes running out of control across the land.

The conflict erupted again in 1459 and York was driven into exile in Ireland. His oldest son Edward, Earl of March, accompanied by his uncle Richard Neville, Earl of Salisbury and Salisbury's son and namesake, the famous Earl of Warwick who is remembered as the Kingmaker, attacked from Calais in 1460 and captured Henry VI. York returned from Ireland and claimed the throne but was forced to accept a compromise agreement in which Henry would remain king for the rest of his life and York would be recognised as his heir. Henry disinherited his own son Edward of Westminster, Prince of Wales but the queen, the indomitable Margaret of Anjou, would not accept the arrangement. Mustering a force in Scotland and pressing south, her forces met those of York at Wakefield, outside Sandal Castle and York, along with his second son Edmund, Earl of Rutland and his brother-in-law Salisbury, was killed. His oldest son, Edward, soon reaped revenge and was proclaimed King Edward IV before marching north to avenge his father and brother at the Battle of Towton, the bloodiest battle ever fought on English soil, at which 28,000 men were reported killed. Edward had two more brothers, George, who he made Duke of Clarence, and Richard, who became Duke of Gloucester and a foundation of Yorkist government. It is this youngest son of York who would become King Richard III, the man who attracts devotion and revulsion in equal measure over half a millennium after his death. How much of each he might deserve will become more evident as we separate fact and fiction.

The remains of Fotheringhay Castle, Northamptonshire, the Yorkist family seat and birthplace of Richard III. (Author's collection)

Chapter 1

A Son of York

Was Richard III the Duke of York?

No. Many mistake references to Richard III's father for references to his youngest son and namesake. Richard, 3rd Duke of York was a great-grandson of King Edward III, whose fourth son Edmund of Langley had been 1st Duke of York. Edmund acted as regent for his nephew Richard II when the king was out of England on several occasions, most notably in 1399 when another nephew, Henry Bolingbroke, returned from exile and claimed the throne for the House of Lancaster. Henry was the oldest son of John of Gaunt, Duke of Lancaster and Edmund's failure to repel his invasion aided the dynastic change from the direct male Plantagenet line to the House of Lancaster as Henry Bolingbroke became King Henry IV.

Edmund's oldest son Edward of Norwich became 2nd Duke of York. Edward had been a favourite of the displaced King Richard II, so he was not widely popular or trusted by the new Lancastrian regime. Edward had been created Duke of Aumale by Richard II, but was stripped of this title on Henry IV's accession and accused of murdering Richard's uncle Thomas, Duke of Gloucester. Edward escaped any punishment but spent the rest of his life under the shadow of suspicion. Fortunately for him, he became friends with Henry IV's oldest son, Prince Henry, fighting alongside him in Wales.

When this prince became King Henry V, Edward accompanied him to France. Perhaps to prove his loyalty, Edward requested the honour of leading the vanguard of Henry's army as it marched across France and of commanding the right wing of the army at the Battle of Agincourt. In his early forties, Edward became the highest profile English casualty of the encounter. Despite two marriages, Edward had no children, and so his prestigious dukedom would pass to another heir.

A plaque in Fotheringhay detailing the children of the House of York born at the castle. (Author collection)

Edward had a younger brother, Richard of Conisburgh, who is something of a mystery. His date of birth has been placed in 1375, but it has also been suggested that he was born as late as 1385. He was also the subject of much gossip, with a rumour circulating that Edmund of Langley, 1st Duke of York was not his birth father, but that his mother, Isabella of Castile had engaged in an affair with John Holland, Duke of Exeter. Richard got no lands or titles from Edward, only being created Earl of Cambridge by Henry V in 1414. As the fleet prepared to set sail for what became the Agincourt Campaign, Henry V got wind of a plan to murder him, and Richard, Earl of Cambridge was implicated. He did not deny his part in what is remembered as the Southampton Plot, so named because Henry was at the port ready to leave when it broke. Richard of Conisburgh, Earl of Cambridge was executed for treason just before the fleet left for a campaign that would also claim the life of his brother.

With both sons of the 1st Duke of York dead, there was only one heir in the male line; Richard of Conisburgh, Earl of Cambridge's only son, the four-year-old Richard, who was now 3rd Duke of York. It would be almost twenty years before he would be declared of age, in 1433, by which time he had also acquired the vast and rich inheritance of his mother's brother, Edmund Mortimer, 5th Earl of March, who had died in 1425. The Mortimer family were descended from the second son of King Edward III, though through a female line, meaning that the Lancastrian kings saw them as a potential threat since they themselves were descended from the third son of King Edward III, John of Gaunt, Duke of Lancaster.

As the focal point of these inheritances of York and Mortimer, Richard, Duke of York was viewed as a potential threat even before he became an adult. He served as Lieutenant-General in France on two occasions, as Lord Lieutenant of Ireland and as Protector of England on two occasions too. He proved himself a competent and capable governor in stark contrast to the weak and ineffectual King Henry VI, his second cousin, once removed. The culmination of all of this was the build-up to and beginning of the period now known as the Wars of the Roses as the country was gripped by faction and suspicion. Richard, Duke of York was killed at the Battle of Wakefield on 30 December 1460 and his titles passed to his own oldest son, Edward, Earl of March. Within a few months, Edward took the crown as King Edward IV, so his time as Edward, Duke of York is forgotten and overlooked.

The youngest son of Richard, Duke of York was also named Richard and would go on to become Duke of Gloucester and then King Richard III, but he was never Duke of York. That title would be passed to Edward IV's youngest son, another Richard, beginning the tradition of creating the monarch's second son as Duke of York. It's easy to see where the confusion arises; Richard III's father was Richard, Duke of York and his nephew was also Richard, Duke of York, but he never was.

Neither is it accurate to call him Richard of York. The royal family did not use a surname at this time, and it was usual to give sons a toponym, a name relating to the place of their birth, instead. Hence, Edmund of Langley had been born at King's Langley, Edward of Norwich in that city and Richard of Conisburgh at Conisburgh Castle. Being a son of a Duke of York did not bestow the sobriquet 'of York'. If a toponym were to be applied to Richard III, it would have been Richard of Fotheringhay.

All of this means that Richard III should not be described as, or confused with, Richard, Duke of York, nor even as Richard of York.

He was never known as Richard of Fotheringhay either, instead being referred to as Richard, Duke of Gloucester after his brother Edward's assent and before becoming king. Before that, he was too young to take part in any matter significant enough to require a form of reference to be created.

Little Known Fact:

The first written reference to the Plantagenet name which is used now for the dynasty that ruled England from 1154 until 1485 appears in the Parliament Rolls in 1460, when Richard III's father, Richard, Duke of York used it as part of his claim to the throne. It must have meant something to people then, but it had never been used in writing to describe the dynasty before.

Glossary:

Medieval armies usually fought using three sections.

The vanguard, or van, was the front section that would join battle first. If arranged in a line across the battlefield, the van would be on the right flank.

The centre, or middle, stood at the centre of the army.

The rearguard, or rear, would be positioned at the back of the rest of the army, or on the left flank of the field.

Was Richard III Born With Physical Disabilities?

Richard III was born on 2 October 1452 at Fotheringhay Castle in Northamptonshire. Fotheringhay was the traditional seat of the Dukes of York, and at the time of his birth, Richard's father was 3rd Duke of York. Named after his father, Richard was the fourth son of his father and mother, Cecily Neville, to survive infancy and he had three older sisters. Richard was to be the last surviving child of the Duke and Duchess, whose oldest child, Anne, was thirteen at the time of her youngest brother's birth.

William Shakespeare's Richard III is a powerful villain who describes himself as 'sent before my time' and 'scarce half made up' at the time of his birth, developing the notion of the character having been born to be

The Church of St Mary and All Saints, Fotheringhay. Richard's great-uncle Edward, Duke of York established a college at the church. It is possible Richard was christened here as it is near to the castle and has a strong family connection. (Author's collection)

A detail from a stained-glass window within St Mary and All Saints Church, Fotheringhay showing the boar badge used by Richard as Duke of Gloucester and king.

evil. Shakespeare did not invent this perception of Richard, though. An antiquarian named John Rous undertook to write a history of the Earls of Warwick during Richard's lifetime and penned the *Rous Roll*, a pro-Yorkist history of England. The original document praised Richard III as a 'good lord' who punished 'oppressors of the commons', but immediately after Henry Tudor's victory at Bosworth, Rous began to scramble around to retrieve copies of his Roll and rewrite sections relating to Richard III in particular.

The reissued version explained that Richard had been born after being 'retained within his mother's womb for two years and emerging with teeth and hair to his shoulders', also noting that he was born under the sign of Scorpio, and 'like a scorpion he combined a smooth front with a stinging tail'. John Rous also described Richard III's appearance as an adult as 'small of stature, with a short face and unequal shoulders, the right higher and the left lower'. The reference to unequal shoulders was long dismissed amongst the other, hugely altered and clearly invented detail that Rous used to try and paper over his previously ardent Yorkist sympathies under the new Tudor regime.

Another source that has been used to point to possible sickliness in Richard as a child is a poem that was written about his siblings, listing the children of the Duke and Duchess of York. The verse was written within a few years of Richard's birth and details all of the couple's children, including those who had not survived infancy. It ends;

> John after William next borne was
> Which both be passed to God's grace.
> George was next, and after Thomas
> Born was, which son after did pace
> By the path of death to the heavenly place.
> Richard liveth yet; but the last of all
> Was Ursula, to Him whom God didst call.

This brief reference to 'Richard liveth yet' has been used to suggest that the boy was sickly and not expected to survive. However, it most likely merely means that Richard was not, at the time of writing, old enough to be deemed free from the risk of infant mortality that had claimed six of his siblings, including the boy born before him, Thomas, and the girl born nearly three years later, Ursula.

The Victorian historian Richard Gairdner, who appears to have been no fan of Richard III's, described him as 'slender and sickly'. He could offer no real evidence of this beyond a reference to a fellow historian, the author of *History of England During the Middle Ages*, who claimed to have 'found evidence somewhere, as he believed, that Richard had serious illness as a child'. The writer added cryptically and unhelpfully that he 'was not able to refer to the source of his information'.

The scoliosis revealed by the examination of Richard III's skeleton is a type that develops during adolescence, so probably began to show when Richard was in his early teens. Apart from this, which seems to have been unknown to most of Richard's contemporaries, there is no evidence at all of any illness or disability affecting Richard from birth or as an infant.

Medieval records of births and childhoods are notoriously scant and poorly kept. Richard's own date of birth is only known definitively because he wrote it in a Book of Hours that he owned. Royal princes and perhaps the first-born sons of senior nobles might be better recorded than most, but by the time even the Duke and Duchess of York welcomed their twelfth child into the world, there was little or no value in recording details of his childhood, his health or his upbringing. As the fourth son of a duke, there would have been little expected of young Richard and not much of the family inheritance to leave to him.

A recently discovered portrait of Richard III dating from the late sixteenth century. Probably part of a panel collection of English monarchs. (Courtesy of Mr J. Mulraine)

Although it is impossible to say with any definitive certainty, there is no evidence that Richard III was sickly, weak or in any way physically disabled as a child. Without medical records, it is impossible to know what minor maladies he may have suffered from, but nothing significant has survived in any record currently known to support the view that he was a sickly child. John Rous's testimony can largely be dismissed, though the reference to uneven shoulders was deemed false along with the rest and turned out to be factual. Nevertheless, two years in the womb seems unlikely and being born with a full set of teeth and shoulder-length hair is almost certainly a fiction created to help ingrain the view of Richard as a man born evil.

To those living during the medieval period, physical disabilities were often, though not always, feared and deemed to be a punishment from God for a corrupt and sinful soul, so giving Richard these outward signs from birth magnifies the evil some writers wished to instil in him. The medieval mind had a tendency to attribute that which it did not understand or could not adequately explain to signs from God. We no longer believe in a correlation between outward appearance and good or evil, so the tools with which these writers sought to make Richard III appear evil should be dismissed too as fictions.

Little known fact:

Richard III is believed to have had four brothers and two sisters who all died in infancy: Joan (born 1438, possible birth, but unconfirmed) Henry (born 1441), William (born 1447), John (born 1448), Thomas (born around 1451) and Ursula (born 1455). Records are frequently unclear or incomplete on these matters, though.

Did Richard III Kill Edmund Beaufort, 2nd Duke of Somerset?

The death of Edmund Beaufort, 2nd Duke of Somerset is the first murder that Richard III is accused of by William Shakespeare. It takes place at the First Battle of St Albans during *Henry VI, Part 2*. In Act V, Scene 2, Richard and Somerset enter fighting and Somerset is killed, after which Richard darkly claims that 'Priests pray for enemies, but princes kill.'

Edmund Beaufort is the name shared by both the 2nd and 4th Dukes of Somerset, the latter being the second son of the former. The father was killed at the First Battle of St Albans and the son after the Battle of Tewkesbury. In Shakespeare's play, Richard also refers to 'The Castle in

Saint Alban's' after killing Somerset, and this reference has some basis in the historical record. A legend, which cannot be proven or disproven, grew up that Edmund Beaufort had been given a prophecy at a fair that he would die beneath the castle. He apparently believed this to mean Windsor Castle and avoided the place at all costs for the rest of his life. Instead, he was reportedly killed beneath the sign outside The Castle Inn at St Albans, the revelation of the true meaning of the prophecy offering him no comfort.

The identity of the one who struck the killing blow on Somerset at St Albans is unknown, as is often the case in battles. The insurmountable problem with attributing this death to the future Richard III is the issue of timing. The First Battle of St Albans took place on 22 May 1455. Richard was born on 2 October 1452, so was only just over two-and-a-half years old when the battle took place. History has ascribed many evil deeds to Richard III, but the thought of a toddler tottering through the streets of St Albans during a battle, brandishing a sword and killing a duke in his late forties is frankly comical.

The fields outside Tewkesbury Abbey where the Battle of Tewkesbury took place on 4 May 1471. (Author's collection)

The plaque marking part of the fields in which Richard fought at the Battle of Tewkesbury 1471. (Author's collection)

The First Battle of St Albans is frequently used as a marker for the beginning of the Wars of the Roses, though in reality there was no dynastic element to the conflict at this point. The issue at stake in 1455 was the right to act as chief advisor to King Henry VI, who had proven himself weak and allowed the country to grow unstable. Factions were rife and out of control and the two leaders of the rival groups, Edmund Beaufort, Duke of Somerset and Richard, Duke of York were not brought to terms. It was Richard III's father who led the forces that ultimately killed this Duke of Somerset, though precisely who landed the fatal blow remains a mystery.

Shakespeare may have written this episode to serve several purposes. He intended Richard III to be the ultimate villain in the play that bore his name and this moment helped to begin the process, to install the character of Richard into the mind of his audience as a killer who lacks compunction. It was also a reference to later events at the Battle of Tewkesbury in 1471, after which Richard, as Constable of England for his brother King Edward IV, oversaw the trial of several Lancastrians who were taken out of Tewkesbury Abbey, including Edmund Beaufort, 4th Duke of Somerset.

During the Battle of Tewkesbury, the only son of King Henry VI, Edward of Westminster, Prince of Wales was killed at the age of seventeen, and Richard III has long been blamed for this death. Shakespeare did not write any part of Edward IV's reign apart from his loss of the throne from 1470-71, after which he moved directly to 1483. The intervening years of Yorkist government under Edward IV are skipped, most likely for political purposes. After all, Elizabeth I was the great-granddaughter of Edward IV, so it was perhaps territory best avoided.

This omission of so much intense and complex politics denied Shakespeare the opportunity to build Richard's character in any subtle or long-term fashion. The scene in which Richard kills Somerset at St Albans serves to bridge the gap, refer to the death of Edward, Prince of Wales at Tewkesbury and establish Richard as a cold-blooded killer before the events of the play *Richard III*. Many of the misconceptions about

The ceiling of Tewkesbury Abbey, redecorated on the orders of Edward IV after the Battle of Tewkesbury. Richard, as Constable, tried the men taken from the Abbey after the battle. The interior was extensively redecorated with Yorkist badges and colours as Edward's way of apologising for removing the defeated Lancastrians from the building. (Author's collection)

Richard III stem from Shakespeare's play, which is a masterpiece in the examination of evil, but which is also fiction. It's like watching Downton Abbey and accepting everything that happens as factually accurate.

It is one of the few absolute certainties about the list of charges lying at Richard III's feet that he did not kill Edmund Beaufort, 2nd Duke of Somerset. No matter how evil anyone believes he was, the notion that he was on the field of battle at the age of two and a half killing a duke is laughable, yet it is a marker of the kind of unreasonable mud that has stuck to his reputation over the centuries. His part in this murder is definitely all fiction.

Little known fact:

Edmund Beaufort, 2nd Duke of Somerset was the mortal enemy of Richard III's father, Richard, Duke of York. After York led an army to Dartford, he was tricked into coming to the king by the news that Edmund had been arrested, only to find that he had not. York was led to London to swear an oath of loyalty to Henry. During the First Protectorate, York had Edmund arrested and placed in the Tower but did not order his execution. St Albans was the culmination of their feud.

Did Richard Meet An Army at the Cross in Ludlow?

There is a legend that at the age of seven, Richard stood on the steps of the market cross in Ludlow with his brother George, his sister Margaret and his mother Cecily to confront a hostile army led by King Henry VI. The story has long added to the notion of his mother as 'Proud Cis', the indomitable Duchess of York, but is there evidence to corroborate this event?

By 1459, Richard's father, the Duke of York, was in open opposition to the government of Henry VI again. Richard, George and Margaret were brought with their mother from the family home at Fotheringhay Castle to the more defensible Ludlow Castle, which sits on the Welsh border and at the heart of a solid block of Marcher lands owned by the Duke of York. York was raising an army at Ludlow and was joined by his brother-in-law Richard Neville, Earl of Salisbury, who had been intercepted on his way and had won the Battle of Blore Heath against an army sent by Queen Margaret. Salisbury's son, the Earl of Warwick also brought a contingent of professional soldiers from the Calais garrison, where Warwick was Captain.

Also at Ludlow were York's two oldest sons, Edward, Earl of March, the future King Edward IV, who was seventeen years old and Edmund, Earl of Rutland who was sixteen. This convergence of the York family is the first time that Richard is recorded as being in the same place as Edward and Edmund and so might represent the first time he met his older brothers. Richard was six years old when he arrived in Ludlow, and the influx of so many men preparing for war must have been an intoxicating site to a boy who might have been too young to understand the politics but was old enough to watch knights and soldiers prepare for war. He may have been in awe of his oldest brother, Edward, who stood 6' 4" tall and was considered something of a giant by the standards of the time.

During the final preparations, Richard passed his seventh birthday on 2 October 1459. Whether it was celebrated in any way is not known, but a few days later, Ludlow was emptied as his father took the army south to Worcester before turning east towards London. As they left Worcester, news arrived that a royal army estimated to be double the size of York's was approaching. Worse still, King Henry himself was riding at the head of the army flying the royal banners. York's plan had probably been to protest against the king's advisors again, but if Henry was at the head of his army, it changed the whole tone of the confrontation. Attacking the king's army would have been treason.

York withdrew to Ludlow, and his army set about constructing earthworks by digging trenches and throwing up the spoil to create earthen ramparts. It was a defensive manoeuvre, but Henry was not pacified. He sent word to the army that any who abandoned York immediately would receive a full pardon, though the Earl of Salisbury was excluded because of his part in the Battle of Blore Heath against the queen's forces. At some point during the late evening or early night, the Calais garrison, led by Andrew Trollope, scaled the earthworks and fled to the king to claim their pardon. The problem for York and his allies was that they took with them details of their numbers, defences and possibly their tactical plans.

An emergency council of war was called, and York, Salisbury, Warwick, Edward and Edmund returned to the castle, instructing their

Ludlow Castle on the Welsh borders, where Richard experienced Yorkist preparations for battle, then was left by his father and older brothers to witness a Lancastrian army sacking the town and castle. (Author's collection)

men to keep their watches and await their return. When the sun rose on 13 October, it became clear that the commanders of the Yorkist army were nowhere to be found. York and his son Edmund had fled into Wales and eventually took a ship to Ireland. His oldest son Edward headed for the south coast with Salisbury and Warwick, finding safety at Calais. Abandoned and leaderless, the Yorkist army submitted to the king.

Henry was not in a forgiving mood and ordered that Ludlow should be sacked as punishment for the support the town had shown its lord. Gregory's Chronicle, written by a Londoner at the time of the events, recorded that 'The misrule of the King's gallants at Ludlow, when they had drunk enough of the wine that was in the taverns and in other places, they full ungodly smote out the heads of the pipes and hogs heads of wine'. He added 'that men went wet shod in wine, and then they robbed the town and bore away bedding, cloth and other goods and defiled many women.'

A story grew up later that Duchess Cecily stood at the market cross with her younger children to bravely confront the royal army as it fell on Ludlow. There is no existing contemporary evidence to confirm this particular event, and it seems to be a myth that evolved later on, though that does not mean there might not be a grain of truth to the story. What is certain is that York had left his wife and three youngest children, thirteen-year-old Margaret, George, who was a few days short of his tenth birthday, and Richard, who had not long passed his seventh, behind when he and the other lords fled. York might have trusted in Henry's honour, and indeed Cecily and the children were seized but placed in the care of her sister the Duchess of Buckingham and remained unharmed as far as can be discerned.

Whether or not Richard stood at the market cross cannot be confirmed. It is clear that as a little boy, he watched in probable excitement as an army swelled within Ludlow, led by his father and two oldest brothers, only to be abandoned by them a matter of days later and left to what must have felt like an uncertain fate as his father's town was ransacked. However the remainder of the York family met the king's men, it must have been a terrifying and uncertain experience for a seven-year-old boy, and it must have left a permanent mark on him as he experienced first-hand just how fragile apparent security could be.

Little known fact:

Richard's brother, Edward IV, is the tallest king ever to have ruled England or Great Britain. At 6'4", he was an inch taller than his grandson Henry VIII and no king before or after has matched his height. Prince William, at 6'3" will come close, but Edward's record looks set to remain in place for a while.

Glossary:

The Marches is a term for a border region and is most often applied to the Welsh or Scottish border areas. Medieval Marcher lords tended to be hard men, operating far from the centre of power on the border of the king's authority.

Pipes and Hogsheads were measures of wine. A hogshead was a large cask containing 63 gallons. A pipe was the second largest measure of wine, after a tun, and contained 126 gallons.

Did Hornby Castle Cost Richard His Life?

As law and order broke down in England in 1469 and continued to unravel into 1470, men of power began to settle slow-moving legal disputes in a more old-fashioned way. Lord Berkley led an army against Lord Lisle at Nibley Green, Gloucestershire on 20 March 1470 in what was to become the last battle between two private armies on English soil to resolve an ongoing argument over an inheritance. The Paston Letters record that the Duke of Norfolk took his cannon to blast the Paston family out of Caister Castle, left to them by the old veteran Sir John Fastolf but coveted by the duke. In the north-west, Richard embroiled himself in one of these disputes with long-lasting consequences.

A bitter feud had been going on for years over the ownership of Hornby Castle between two of the most prominent families in the region. The castle had been owned by Sir Thomas Harrington, the son of Sir William Harrington, Henry V's standard bearer at the Battle of Agincourt. Sir Thomas had been killed at the Battle of Wakefield in 1460 alongside Richard's father, the Duke of York. Also amongst the casualties was Thomas's oldest son John, who was survived by two young daughters. Crucially, the reports from the battlefield stated that Sir Thomas died during the fighting and that John died after the battle of his wounds. This meant that on Thomas's death, John inherited, however briefly and that on John's passing, his daughters inherited. Once married, the land and wealth held by the girls would pass to their husbands and out of the Harrington family.

John's younger brothers, James and Robert, claimed that John had died before their father, so the inheritance rightly belonged to James. This was most likely a desperate lie to keep control of the land, but the brothers took their nieces and withdrew behind the walls of Hornby Castle. In 1468, King Edward called the brothers before the Court of Chancery to answer for their behaviour and Thomas, Lord Stanley petitioned for the wardship of the girls and was granted it. Stanley immediately married both sisters into his own family and laid claim to Hornby Castle. Much like the Paston family at Caister Castle, the Harrington brothers refused to leave Hornby.

Thomas Stanley's family owned vast swaths of land across Cheshire and North Wales and had been expanding voraciously since the days of

Thomas's grandfather Sir John. With his younger brother Sir William, Thomas was continuing to grow the Stanley portfolio and influence. Hornby Castle, a beautiful property perched above the valley of the River Lune, stood on Stanley's frontier and would make a fantastic addition to their holdings. In contrast to the Harringtons, the Stanley family had contrived to miss the Battle of Wakefield. The family's allegiances were never clear, and they had perfected the careful art of walking a tightrope, offering no real commitment but burning no bridges either. Nevertheless, Edward IV found in their favour and ordered the Harrington brothers to surrender the castle. Ever the pragmatist, Edward recognised the power the Stanley brothers could wield. They were famous for being able to raise a considerable number of men; and even if he couldn't make them fight for him, Edward had an interest in making sure they didn't fight against him.

As disorder began to grip the country, the dispute over the ownership of Hornby Castle was one which Lord Stanley decided to avoid waiting for legal action to resolve. He ordered a giant cannon known as Mile Ende to be transported from Bristol to Hornby for the express purpose of blasting the Harrington brothers out of the castle they still refused to surrender. No shot was ever fired, though, and there is only one explanation for Lord Stanley's failure to bring the matter to a close.

On 26 March 1470, Richard, Duke of Gloucester issued a warrant which was crucially signed 'at Hornby'. The seventeen-year-old younger brother of the king had placed himself inside Hornby Castle, effectively daring Lord Stanley to fire at him. It is interesting to consider the choice that Richard made. He has been held up as a paragon of loyalty to his brother Edward, but in this case, we can see him openly defying the king's will. The Harrington family had come from the north with the Earl of Salisbury to support the Yorkist cause in 1459, Sir Thomas and his second son James had fought and been captured at the Battle of Blore Heath and Sir Thomas, with his oldest son John, had given their lives at Wakefield. The Stanley family's record was a little more sketchy. There is some evidence that Sir William Stanley fought with Salisbury at Blore Heath, though Thomas Stanley had been summoned to fight for the royal army and failed to arrive. They had been notably absent at Wakefield too.

Legally, Hornby Castle belonged to the Stanley family. The laws of inheritance were usually considered sacrosanct, though Edward IV was not above setting them aside when it suited him. In this instance, it suited him to uphold the rules that meant Hornby belonged to the Thomas Stanley. Richard clearly saw it differently, apparently ignoring these rules and preferring a form of natural justice that would see the Harrington family rewarded for their steadfast loyalty by retaining the family property they should have lost.

The real effect of this was probably to make an enemy of Lord Stanley. Fifteen years later, as Lord Stanley looked down at the field of the Battle of Bosworth and tried to decide whose side to take, it is entirely possible that Richard's actions at Hornby were a factor in the final decision to help Henry Tudor take Richard's crown. It is an early demonstration of Richard's lack of the political pragmatism that characterised his brother's reign and perhaps tells us a good deal about the character of this future king.

Little known fact:

Stanley family legend holds that Lord Stanley's forces met those of Richard, Duke of Gloucester at the Battle of Ribble Bridge in 1470. Not only did Lord Stanley reportedly win, but he captured Richard's standard, a prize that was kept on display at Wigan Church until the Reformation. There is no official record of this battle, so it remains unclear whether it actually took place or not.

Chapter 2

Regaining The Kingdom

Did Richard Get His First Taste of Battle at Barnet?

Following Edward IV's triumphal return to England after his expulsion in 1470, he placed Henry VI back into custody at the Tower of London and quickly regained control of the capital. Warwick's brother, George Neville, Archbishop of York had allowed Edward back into the city and handed the beleaguered and perhaps bewildered Lancastrian king over. The Earl of Warwick himself, who had facilitated the Lancastrian readeption, was still in the Midlands with a large force and Edward knew that he had to deal with his cousin once and for all if he was to be secure on his throne.

King Edward collected his family from the sanctuary at Westminster Abbey, including his first son, also named Edward, who had been born while the king was out of the country. The reunion was brief as Edward gathered as many men as possible and marched north out of London to meet Warwick. The armies drew close on the evening of 13 April 1471 just outside Barnet and made their camps. Warwick ordered his cannon to fire throughout the night but the two armies had camped closer to each other than they thought and the king's guns remained silent as Warwick overshot their location all night.

In the morning, there was thick fog, and the two armies lined up too close to each other and off centre so that the right wings of each force jutted out beyond the opposing left. Richard had been given command of the right flank, facing the Duke of Exeter. Edward's friend Lord Hastings was on the left flank, facing the Earl of Oxford, and Edward held the centre against Warwick and his brother Lord Montagu. When the armies engaged, Oxford quickly routed Hastings' men and chased them back to Barnet. At the same time, Richard easily drove Exeter's force back.

In the centre, the fighting was hard and evenly balanced. After a while, Oxford's men returned to the field from pursuing Hastings' flank, and it was this that reportedly caused chaos. Oxford's banner displayed a star with rays, and when it appeared back on the right flank of Warwick's army, it was mistaken in the fog and commotion for King Edward's banner of a sun in splendour, which also had rays radiating from it. Warwick's men unleashed a panicked volley of arrows at Oxford's men, who cried treason in an infectious terror that ran rampant through the army and caused men to flee the battlefield. Warwick himself was pursued into Wrotham Wood where he was cut down, despite an order Edward had reportedly given that he should be taken alive.

This is Richard's first officially reported involvement in a battle. The only other possible occasion on which he may have been on the battlefield is at the Battle of Ribble Bridge before he had left England with his brother, but this battle only seems to appear in Stanley family legend. Richard was eighteen years old at the Battle of Barnet, and although this might have been his first engagement, he would have been preparing for it since childhood. Details of Richard's education have not been preserved, but martial preparation was considered every bit as important as an education in numeracy and literacy. Richard would have been trained in the use of sword and mace amongst other weapons and would have been taught to ride, wear armour and understand military tactics from a young age.

Richard's involvement in this battle might have been made significantly easier by the misalignment of the armies at Barnet. It meant that he didn't face the more intense fighting in the centre, though in the confusion of the mist and the overlapping armies, it held its own challenges. As a first experience of battle, it might have taught Richard about the uncertainty of the field and the need to adapt quickly. The misunderstanding that had caused Warwick's army to flee would only have reinforced those lessons.

One important consideration is the impact that Richard's scoliosis may have had on his martial prowess. From his early teens, the condition would have become progressively worse, and the curvature of his spine would have caused pressure on his lungs, making him breathless more quickly and less able to sustain the physical exertion demanded on the battlefield. It is likely that Richard's armour would have required adaptation to compensate for the unevenness in his shoulders, yet despite all of the potential impacts of his scoliosis, Richard appears to have acquitted himself well at Barnet and doesn't seem to have been hindered. His competence as a soldier would become a large part of Richard's reputation and the discovery of his remains that confirmed the presence of scoliosis cast doubt on his ability to take part in battles. It is clear from the sources that Richard was involved in the Battle of Barnet and that he distinguished himself for his talent rather than any hindrance.

It is true, as far as can be discerned, that Richard's first taste of battle came at Barnet on 13 April 1471 and that he acquitted himself well. He had prepared for that moment for years, ironically under the auspices of Richard Neville, the Earl of Warwick, who was his opponent in this battle.

Little known fact:

The Duke of Exeter who led Warwick's left flank at Barnet was Henry Holland, the third duke. He had been married to Richard's sister Anne but had been attainted in 1461 for siding with the Lancastrians and had separated from his wife. He was, therefore, the ex-brother-in-law of King Edward IV and Richard.

Glossary:

Readeption is the word invented by Parliament in 1470 for the reinstatement of a formerly deposed king. It had not happened since the Conquest, and no one knew what to call it, so the word readeption was created.

Did Richard Kill Edward of Westminster?

On 4 May 1471, in scorching hot weather, the armies of the Yorkist king Edward IV met those of the Lancastrian forces gathered by Margaret of Anjou in the names of her husband, the ousted prisoner King Henry VI, and her son, the seventeen-year-old Edward of Westminster, Prince of Wales. This is a murder Richard, himself only eighteen years old, has long been blamed for, but can he really be found guilty based on the evidence available?

After impressing his brother at the Battle of Barnet several weeks earlier, Richard was given control of the vanguard of Edward's army, placed on the right wing. Edward himself controlled the centre, and his close friend Lord Hastings had the rear, or left wing. On the Lancastrian side, Edmund Beaufort, Duke of Somerset, a member of the same Beaufort family that were entrenched in a deep and long-running feud with the House of York, had command of the vanguard. Lord Wenlock commanded the centre, where Edward, Prince of Wales had been permitted to take a position by his mother in the hope that he would inspire their men as well as gain some valuable experience. John Courtenay, Earl of Devon held the Lancastrian left, acting as a rear guard.

The battle opened, as was traditional, with a volley of arrows and a thunderous round of cannon fire. Somerset realised that the Yorkists far outgunned the Lancastrian army at range, so moved his vanguard to try and flank King Edward's centre. The manoeuvre failed, and Somerset was driven back towards Richard's vanguard. In a panic, the Lancastrians began to flee, some drowning in the nearby river and others being pursued by Richard's men towards Tewkesbury Abbey. The battle was a close-run thing for a long time before the Yorkists secured victory; and as the dust settled, it became clear that the seventeen-year-old Lancastrian Prince of Wales was amongst the dead.

In *Henry VI, Part 3*, Shakespeare has the three brothers of York, King Edward, George and Richard take it in turns to stab the prince after he insults them all. *Holinshed's Chronicle*, first published in 1577 and a source used by Shakespeare, claims that Richard struck the first blow against the Prince. In his *Anglica Historia*, Polydore Vergil, wrote at the opening if the fifteenth century that George, Richard and Lord Hastings captured the young man and then murdered him together.

The most contemporary source available is *The Arrivall of King Edward IV*, an account of the reclamation of the Yorkist throne written by an anonymous chronicler who at least appears to have been an eyewitness to the events he describes, though his bias is plain to see. *The Arrivall* merely records that Prince Edward was 'slayne in the field', giving no name to his killer or special mention to his fall. *Warkworth's Chronicle* is considered more Lancastrian in sympathy but was written at the time of the battle. This writer asserts that it was Richard's brother George who captured Prince Edward and, ignoring his pleas for mercy, orders his summary execution on a makeshift block.

This particular version of events is interesting. George had been wrapped up in Warwick's revolt, the original aim of which was to place George on the throne and as part of which George had married Warwick's eldest daughter Isabel Neville. When Warwick had subsequently agreed to an alliance with Margaret of Anjou, the plan had altered, aiming to put Henry VI back on the throne with his son, Prince Edward, as his heir. George was promised the crown if Prince Edward died childless, but he was suddenly significantly relegated. Prince Edward had been married to Isabel's sister, Anne Neville (who would later become Richard's wife), so the young men were brothers-in-law. George may well have had an axe to grind with the man who had stolen his chance of the crown – not to mention the fact that Prince Edward's death made George the legitimate heir of Henry VI and the House of Lancaster.

The most impartial version of the events probably appears in the *Crowland Chronicle*, which notes that '...there were slain on the queen's side, either in the field or after the battle, by the avenging hands of certain persons, Prince Edward, the only son of King Henry...', before giving a list of other notable casualties. The reference is annoyingly vague but seems to suggest that the anonymous writer of the *Crowland Chronicle* felt Prince Edward was killed deliberately by 'the avenging hands of certain persons', which further suggests that he knew who the killer – or killers – were, but did not want to name him, or them.

Richard is further excused from suspicion by the accounts of the battle that have him pursuing Somerset's routed vanguard towards the town, meaning that he would not have been in the field if Prince Edward was killed during the fighting. Given that Prince Edward was in the Lancastrian centre, opposite King Edward's centre, where George was also posted, it seems they might be the more likely candidates for exacting revenge for their father's death at Wakefield.

It remains possible that Prince Edward was cut down in the general melee by a man-at-arms. If he were sought out on the battlefield by one of the Yorkist leaders, then it would have been a natural tactic given his position and presence on the field. If Prince Edward had been captured and executed in the immediate aftermath of the battle, he can hardly have expected any other fate having lost to an implacable enemy. The fate of Prince Edward's father was about to demonstrate as much.

Although it remains impossible to conclude that Richard definitely had nothing to do with the death of Prince Edward at Tewkesbury, the contemporary accounts seem to make it unlikely that he was on the field when it happened. It is an accusation that was later woven into the developing reputation of Richard as a ruthless, evil murderer. Even if he was involved in some way, it was probably a natural consequence of the battle that Prince Edward would die once he had lost the field. It has become convenient to lay the blame at the tip of Richard's sword, but it is most likely a fiction that he killed Edward of Westminster, Prince of Wales.

Little known fact:

The sacristy door of Tewkesbury Abbey is lined with horse armour recovered from the battlefield by the monks. It still bears the puncture marks of arrows that pierced it on 4 May 1471 in an eerie reminder of its provenance.

Did Richard III Kill Henry VI?

Following the Battle of Tewkesbury, at which the Lancastrian Prince of Wales, the only heir to King Henry VI's throne, had been killed, Edward IV returned to London, arriving in triumph at the head of around 30,000 men on 21 May 1471. The following morning, the death of King Henry VI was solemnly reported throughout the City, and ever since, the involvement of Richard in the death has been mooted. Is this one murder we can be confident Richard committed?

Shakespeare has his Richard commit the act on stage in *Henry VI, Part 3*. He visits Henry in his cell, and after Richard tries to convince Henry he is not there to kill him: 'Think'st thou I am an executioner?', we are provided with more evidence of Richard's malice by the very fact that the meek, pliable and simple Henry can see right through him: 'If murdering innocents be executing, Why, then thou art an executioner.'

When Richard taunts Henry that he killed the former king's son 'for his presumption', Henry berates Richard for his evil nature and the ill omens of his birth. The king tells him 'The owl shriek'd at thy birth, -an evil sign; The night-crow cried, aboding luckless time; Dogs howl'd, and hideous tempest shook down trees; The raven rook'd her on the chimney's top,' adding 'To wit, an indigested and deformed lump, Not like the fruit of such a goodly tree. Teeth hadst thou in thy head when thou wast born, To signify thou camest to bite the world'. At this point, Richard plunges his knife into Henry and kills him, adding a second thrust as he ruthlessly adds 'If any spark of life be yet remaining, Down, down to hell; and say I sent thee thither'.

The purpose of this episode in Shakespeare's telling of the Wars of the Roses is clear; it sets the tone for the play *Richard III* but also shows the audience that even one as devoid of worldly wisdom as Henry can see Richard's evil. The series of early murders, beginning with Somerset, including Edward of Westminster and ending in this play with Henry VI, establish Richard as a callous killer. As he drags Henry's lifeless body away, he reveals the entire premise of the production *Richard III*, ominously intoning: 'King Henry and the prince his son are gone: Clarence, thy turn is next, and then the rest, Counting myself but bad till I be best.'

The Tudor antiquary Robert Fabyan, writing in the early sixteenth century, asserted that 'the most common fame went, that he was stuck with a dagger by the hands of the Duke of Gloucester'. Polydore Vergil, at around the same time, wrote that 'the continual report is, that Richard duke of Gloucester killed him with a sword,' adding, importantly, 'whereby his brother might be delivered from all fear of hostility'.

Warkworth's Chronicle is a contemporary source and records that Henry died between 11 o'clock and midnight on 21 May 1471, 'being then in the Tower the Duke of Gloucester, brother to King Edward, and many other'. Warkworth is perhaps deliberately careful to implicate Richard without openly accusing him, and if so, he may have been wise to be so vague. The official Yorkist version of the events of that night appears in *The Arrival of King Edward IV*, which insists that Henry died 'of pure displeasure and melancholy' at the news of the death of his son and the final loss of his cause. It is perhaps too easy to completely discount this version since Henry had been in poor health for almost twenty years by this point and a prisoner in the Tower for several years before the readeption. He may have suffered a stroke or heart attack at the news, though it perhaps remains a little too convenient to ring true.

Henry had been kept alive this long because of the existence of his young son. With a youthful, dynamic heir, the Lancastrian cause might have been reinvigorated by the death of the old king, but Henry remained a sorry figure with little interest in challenging for the crown, and he was also a figure who could easily be blamed for the civil unrest since the 1450's. His son's death probably sealed Henry's fate. Richard might well have been intimately involved in the demise of the former king, as it was a complex matter. Who could Edward trust to kill a king, even a deposed one? Allowing a commoner, or even a noble, to do it would set a dangerous precedent for regicide. A brother of the king who was in a position of complete trust might have been one of the few people able to carry out the act. At the same time, Richard was Lord High Constable of England, appointed in 1469 for life. The Constable was responsible for law and order and for protecting the king from treason and other threats. As such, Richard might have been the natural choice to oversee the killing of the former king, even if he didn't deliver the fatal blow himself.

The fate of Henry VI remains too unclear to point the finger at Richard with certainty, but of all the crimes he is frequently accused of, this might be one in which his involvement is more likely than most, perhaps even more likely than not. He was at the Tower when it happened, according to Warkworth's report, though so were many others. His responsibility for justice and security along with his position as Edward's brother might have made him the only person Edward would select to carry out the act.

If Henry was killed, and even if Richard delivered the blow himself, it was undoubtedly all done at the express command of King Edward IV. Edward was the one who gained from Henry's death, not Richard. As Vergil stated, if Richard did it, it was so that 'his brother might be delivered from all fear of hostility' and if Richard had killed such a high-profile figure without instruction, Edward is unlikely to have trusted him as much as he did for the next decade or more. Ultimately, responsibility for the death of Henry VI probably lies with Edward IV.

Little known fact:

There is a plaque on the floor of the Wakefield Tower of the Tower of London that reads 'By Tradition Henry VI died here May 21 1471'.

It is within a small chapel where the former king was supposedly at prayer when he was murdered, though as we have seen, there is little real evidence to support this assertion.

Glossary:

Regicide is the murder of a king. A person who kills a king is also known as a regicide. It derives from the Latin regis, meaning 'of king', and cida, meaning 'killer', or cidium, meaning 'killing'.

Chapter 3

In The North

Was Richard III's Marriage a Love Match?

Primarily, almost all marriages amongst the nobility were a matter of political alliance and advancement. Love was always a secondary consideration, and although both parties might hope that love would grow from a union, it was by no means considered a requirement. One notable and contemporary exception was the marriage of Edward IV to Elizabeth Woodville, which brought no political advantage to the new king and seems to have been made from either love, lust or a combination of the two.

Richard married Anne Neville, the younger of the two daughters of Richard Neville, Earl of Warwick. The precise date of the marriage is unknown, but it was probably during 1472. Warwick had rebelled against Edward IV and taken over England in the name of the deposed Lancastrian King Henry VI for a short time before Edward returned and reclaimed his throne. At the Battle of Barnet on 14 April 1471, Warwick was killed fighting against Edward, and the powerful earl left no son as his heir but had two daughters. The eldest daughter, Isabel, had been married to Richard's brother George, Duke of Clarence as part of Warwick's uprising and although George was now back in the fold, Edward must have been worried about the prospect of George acquiring the vast estates and wealth of the Neville family.

Crucially, Richard Neville was not attainted, so his lands would pass to his daughters. A legend later emerged that George and Isabel kept Anne hidden away in London, working as a kitchen maid, to prevent her from marrying and claiming her half of the inheritance – or at least, to stop her husband claiming it. Richard supposedly tracked Anne down and gallantly rescued the damsel in distress from the kitchens so that they could be

married. There is little evidence
of this story, and it appears to
be a later myth that has grown
up, though it may be telling
that amongst all the stories of
Richard's evil machinations,
this tale of chivalry has survived.

Unless it was not chivalry
at all. Even with just half of the
Neville inheritance, Anne was a
huge dynastic prize. Her father
had previously arranged her
marriage to Henry VI's son and
heir Edward, Prince of Wales as
part of his rebellion; but with
his death at Tewkesbury, Anne,
and her share of the inheritance,
became available again. For
Richard, it represented the
most significant opportunity
for power and for Edward,
it would dilute George's potentially immense resources and authority;
critical given his recent part in the Lancastrian revival.

Anne, Queen of Richard III.

Queen Anne Neville, wife of Richard III and youngest daughter of Richard Neville, Earl of Warwick, the Kingmaker. (Courtesy of British Library)

Eventually, Edward IV used Parliament to divide the Warwick
inheritance between his brothers, giving Isabel, and therefore George,
the Midlands and West Country portions while handing Richard, de jure
uxoris, the northern power base of the Neville family. Richard has been
criticised as cruel because as part of the settlement, Isabel and Anne's
mother, Warwick's widow Anne Beauchamp was declared legally dead
so her lands could be shared out too. The lack of attainder meant that
property could not be seized by the crown and both George and Richard
appear to have campaigned to avoid such a measure, preferring to hold
their new lands and titles by right of inheritance rather than by the king's
grace. The law of inheritance was strict, ancient and kings ignored it at
their peril, but if Edward took the lands and gave them to his brothers,
they could be taken back just as easily.

Edward circumvented this by adding a clause to both brothers' inheritance that essentially meant that they lost everything if the line of Warwick's nearest male heir, his nephew, George Neville, was broken. George was effectively being deprived of any share of the inheritance but was created Duke of Bedford and promised a marriage to one of Edward IV's daughters in compensation. The measure was designed to protect the Neville male line but would eventually add fuel to political problems a decade later. It is clear that Anne represented a powerful dynastic and political advantage to both Richard and Edward.

None of that necessarily precludes a love match, though. Richard had grown up in the household of Anne's father, and it is likely that the two knew each other, though Anne was some four years Richard's junior. There is clear evidence that they sat together at a feast at least once. In 1465, Richard was still in Warwick's household as Duke of Gloucester. He attended the feast to celebrate the enthronement of Warwick's younger brother George as Archbishop of York, a huge event, the seating plan for which is preserved. Richard, Duke of Gloucester was seated at a table with his sister Elizabeth, Duchess of Suffolk, with the Countess of Northumberland and with Isabel and Anne Neville. We can, therefore, place them with certainty at the same feast, sitting at the same table in 1465.

The couple were married for over ten years and had one son together. There is no evidence that they were distant from one another, but neither is there contemporary evidence of a great love match. This is generally inferred from the length and apparent contentedness of their union. The Crowland Chronicler wrote that when news of the death of their son reached Richard and Anne, 'at Nottingham, where they were then residing, you might have seen his father and mother in a state almost bordering on madness, by reason of their sudden grief'. The implication is that they took solace in one another's company.

Later biographers have asserted that Richard shed tears at his wife's funeral, but there is no account of him attending the funeral or shedding tears. These seem to be flourishes added later. Richard himself stated when refuting the rumour that he had poisoned his wife, that he was not 'willyng or glad of the dethe of his quene but as sorye & in hert as hevye as man myght be'.

It is impossible to tell what goes on behind closed doors; more so behind those closed half a millennium ago. There is circumstantial evidence to suggest that the marriage between Richard and Anne was happy and perhaps filled with love, but there was also a dynastic benefit to the union to both. It is perhaps a case of balance, an instance in which a political match carried an element of personal attachment that became love.

Little known fact:

As well as the seating plan at the feast Richard attended in 1465, the list of food prepared has survived and is pretty eye-watering. It included 104 oxen, 1,000 muttons, 400 swans, 204 cranes, 2,000 chickens, 1,000 capons, 2,000 geese, 2,000 pigs, 500 stags, 4,000 venison pastries, 2,400 sandpipers and 4,000 ducks. If there was any room for pudding, guests could choose from 4,000 baked tarts, 3,000 baked custards and 2,000 hot custards amongst other things. A few belts might have needed loosening after that.

Glossary:

De jure uxoris is a Latin legal term meaning 'by right of his wife'. When an inheritance went to a female heir, it would in practice be controlled by her husband before passing to their children, if they had any. Richard Neville was Earl of Warwick de jure uxoris because he acquired the Warwick lands and titles from the inheritance of his wife.

Was Richard All Nice?

Traditional history, in a line firmly led by Shakespeare's hobbling villain, offers Richard no good qualities to speak of. The Bard made him funny and oddly charming, but only to facilitate his evil motives. At the other end of the scale, many revisionists have tried to paint Richard as nothing short of a hero whose every deed can be polished until it gleams. The truth, as it usually does, lies somewhere in the middle. Medieval politics, amongst those high enough on the social ladder for the fall below them to look frightening, was often brutal and cutthroat. It would have been hard for any royal duke living through a period of civil upheaval like the

Wars of the Roses to retain and strengthen his position without getting his hands dirtied. Richard certainly didn't avoid it.

After Edward IV had regained his throne in 1471, Richard married Anne Neville, the younger daughter of the Kingmaker Earl of Warwick, whose elder daughter Isabel was married to Richard's brother George. When it came to carving up the Neville inheritance, things got ugly very quickly. Richard and George both pressed their brother the king not to attaint Warwick, but to allow them to inherit the lands and titles he had held legally. The advantage of this for the brothers is clear; if Edward seized them and gifted them, Richard and George would hold them from the king and might lose them as quickly as they had been granted them. Obtaining them under the laws of inheritance gave them a firmer grip, though Edward was to show that he was happy to ride roughshod over the laws of inheritance when it suited him.

When the dust settled, Richard was given the northern heart of the Neville patrimony and George the lands in the Midlands and south-west that had Warwick as their power base. However, the brothers had not got everything their own way. Edward inserted a clause in the Parliamentary grants to both his brothers that tied their title to the live and issue of George Neville, the Earl of Warwick's nephew, who would otherwise have been his male heir. If George Neville died or if his male line failed, the claims of both Richard and George would revert to a life interest only. This measure was claimed to be for the protection of young George Neville, but it was also Edward's way of subverting his brother's wishes. It was a measure that would prove devastating in 1483.

Warwick's widow Anne Beauchamp, through whose line Warwick had inherited the title he was known by, was still alive and entitled not only to her dower but also had a claim to the Beauchamp inheritance in her own right. Edward swiftly overcame this 'problem' by having Anne declared legally dead in Parliament and her property divided between her daughters' husbands as if she was really dead. Although this is definitely the king at work, Richard undoubtedly profited from this ugly episode. The northern Neville lands became his power base and his home for a decade.

There was another example of Richard's ruthless streak in 1471 when his brother Edward IV also granted him the lands of John de Vere, Earl

The Great Hall at Middleham Castle, where Richard entertained guests. The castle offers commanding views of the surrounding landscape. (Author's collection)

A statue of Richard III within Middleham Castle. (Author's collection)

of Oxford, who was, at the time, a fugitive after the fall of the Lancastrian readeption. Oxford was acting like a pirate in the Channel, and the king seized his properties and gifted them to Richard. Oxford's mother, Elizabeth Howard, had her dower, one-third of the lands, and was an heiress in her own right as a Howard, the family that would later become Dukes of Norfolk. In 1473, Richard harassed the dowager countess, who was by then in her early sixties, until she signed over her share of the Oxford estates as well as her own inheritance. Elizabeth had been living in a nunnery at Stratford le Bow, from which Richard's men took her to Stepney and, according to what the countess reportedly told one of her feoffees, Henry Robson, threatened to move her to the freezing northern fortress of Middleham Castle, where she feared the cold would kill her.

After being moved once more to Walbroke, the dowager countess signed all of her estates over to Richard. She also reportedly told Henry Robson that 'she was sorry that she for saving her life had disheritt her heirs'. Once more, it must be acknowledged that Richard was acting with the express authority of the king. Edward had granted the lands to Richard and probably told him that if he wanted the enjoyment of them, he would have to go and take them for himself. However, Richard's actions were both ruthless and, if the reports are to be believed, verging on cruel to an elderly lady. To balance that view further, though, this was an old lady providing support to her son, a rebel, a fugitive, a pirate and an intractable enemy of Edward IV.

When Henry VII came to power, Oxford was the commander of his army and was immediately restored to favour. In Henry's first Parliament in November 1485, Oxford petitioned for the return of his and his mother's lands. Elizabeth had passed away a decade earlier, but Oxford was keen to have her ill-treatment put on record. He insisted that she 'was so threatened, put in fear of her life and imprisoned by Richard III' that 'for fear and by means of the same, the same countess, in order to save her life, was compelled' to hand over everything to Richard.

Richard was not all nice. He could not have been a successful nobleman in the late fifteenth century if he had been all nice. It is worth considering whether his means were any more unsavoury than those of his contemporaries, and during a period of such upheavals and shifting alliances, they were probably not all that remarkable. Edward was undoubtedly behind these moves, authorising them and possibly even egging Richard on, but it must be acknowledged that Richard was willing to mistreat potentially vulnerable women to make sure he got what he wanted. Any version of Richard that is entirely evil or wholly nice is a fiction.

Little known fact:

A dower was a central principle in English law for the provision of a wife should she be widowed. It could be set at the time of a marriage or by the law when a husband died and was generally one-third of the lands held by the husband when he died. These were placed in trust for his widow to provide for her during her lifetime and on her death, would revert back to the main estate.

Glossary:

Feoffees were those granted the freehold of land or property, usually by a powerful noble. Enfeoffment was effectively a medieval form of tax avoidance since the nobleman would retain real ownership and the income from lands without appearing, on paper, to own them.

Did Richard Defy His Brother At Picquigny?

In 1475, Edward IV launched an invasion of France in alliance with Charles the Bold, Duke of Burgundy. When the large English army landed, Charles was nowhere to be seen having decided to head off east to attack a remote town. The French King Louis XI, known as the Universal Spider for the webs of intrigue he weaved, saw his chance to end the invasion quickly and offered Edward IV a financial package he knew the English king would not be able to turn down. Richard, though, was reportedly less impressed.

King Edward took the bait, and the two kings met on a specially erected bridge at Picquigny, just outside Amiens, separated by a wooden grill to prevent any assignation attempts. Louis had judged Edward's lack of motivation and will to pursue the invasion perfectly. France would pay England 75,000 crowns to leave the country immediately and an annual pension of 50,000 crowns per years, a significant figure for the English king. Louis further agreed to pay a ransom of 50,000 crowns for Margaret of Anjou, the widow of Henry VI and many of Edward's nobles and advisors also accepted hefty pensions to go along with the peace. His closest friend Lord Hastings took 2,000 crowns a year, John Howard received 1,200 crowns, the Chancellor Thomas Rotherham, Bishop of Lincoln and later Archbishop of York got 1,000 crowns a year and John Morton, Bishop of Ely profited to the tune of 600 crowns a year.

Philip de Commines was an eyewitness to the events at Picquigny and the subsequent celebrations in Amiens, and he described the events in detail in his *Memoirs*. He noted that 'The Duke of Gloucester, the King of England's brother, and some other persons of quality, were not present at this interview, as being averse to the treaty'. It seems that Richard and others saw the swift capitulation and agreement of terms as dishonourable bribes.

As the treaty was signed at Picquigny, Edward's other brother, the wayward George, Duke of Clarence was at Edward's side, and it must have appeared odd and perhaps concerning that the usually dependable

Edward IV meets Louis XI of France at Picquigny. Richard did not attend the signing of the treaty and it is believed that this was because he disagreed with his brother's policy. (From James Doyle's A Chronicle of England, *via Wikimedia Commons)*

Richard was the absent one. As the events surrounding Hornby Castle had shown in 1470, Richard was clearly not averse to openly opposing his brother the king when he felt the cause was just. His failure to attend the signing of the Treaty of Picquigny would have been something like a diplomatic incident, and it would have been publicly embarrassing for Edward.

Louis well-deserved his epithet of the Universal Spider. Threads of his web would have jangled when Richard made himself known by his defiance. de Commines added that Richard did attend the celebrations at Amiens after the Treaty was concluded, noting that 'they recollected themselves afterwards, and the Duke of Gloucester waited on the king our master at Amiens, where he was splendidly entertained, and nobly presented both with plate and fine horses'. King Louis would keep a close eye on Richard over the years that followed, having no doubt identified him as a less pliable figure than his brother Edward.

When Edward and his army returned to England, there was general disapproval of the Treaty of Picquigny. Many of those who had joined the king as well as those at home had stumped up a lot of money to fund the expedition and now had no return on their investment, not even in honour. Richard's public opposition to the terms and his refusal to accept a bribe or a pension from Louis XI must have been more popular amongst those at home that Edward's capitulation.

Richard is traditionally viewed as utterly loyal to his brother Edward, yet this episode demonstrates that he was not always blindly obedient. When Richard perceived his brother to be in the wrong, he was not afraid to make his feelings clear, even at the risk of embarrassing his brother in front of the King of France. Richard's own lack of political guile is perhaps visible here too. In marking himself out to the French king, Richard might well have believed he acted with honour and in the spirit of the campaign, unlike those who accepted Edward's peace and Louis's bribes, but he also made sure he was noticed for the wrong reasons. One unforeseen consequence was that when Richard took the throne of England, he already had a reputation in France as one who was interested in pursuing war and who could not be bought off as easily as his brother had been. This reputation would play into the French reaction to Richard's accession to the throne as they suffered from their own internal crisis and viewed the possible threat represented by Richard as incredibly dangerous.

It is true that Richard defied his brother King Edward at Picquigny in 1475. He demonstrated open opposition to his brother's decision to accept King Louis XI's peace terms and the financial incentives that accompanied it. Richard's failure to attend the signing of the Treaty, as his other brother George did, would have been a very noticeable snub to Edward. King Louis's subsequent interest in Richard is easy to understand from a king famous for knowing his friends and his enemies as well as he possibly could. The episode is at odds with Richard's reputation as utterly loyal, though he might perhaps have expressed his opposition to the Treaty as being born of loyalty. Certainly, he doesn't seem to have been afraid to tell his brother the king when he believed him to be in the wrong.

In France, Richard's card was well and truly marked, too.

Little known fact:

The English envoy to Spain, Louis de Bretaylle, was reported to have complained of the Treaty of Picquigny that in that single act, Edward had ruined his reputation and destroyed the honour of all his previous victories. This would demonstrate the popularity of Richard's stance, even if it turned out to be politically damaging in the long run.

Why Was Richard So Loved In The North?

Richard has long enjoyed a close association with Yorkshire that stems from his time as Duke of Gloucester when he effectively managed the northern parts of England for his brother. The dichotomy between this man and one who would murder his nephews to snatch the crown is part of the reason that many refute the existence of the latter. So why did, and does, this region seem to hold Richard so dear?

The north-south divide in England was far starker during the medieval period than it is today. Southerners tended to view their northern cousins as a different race, far more like the uncultured Scots than themselves. Their accents made many in the south think they spoke another language altogether and they were, to some extent, feared as a military threat. In the north, the distance from London and the centre of royal authority meant that, depending on the nature, ability and interests of the king, the north was almost an independent region. Lords found the freedom to operate out of sight of the king's gaze, but the area also felt disconnected in political and financial terms; a second-class region compared to the wealthier south.

In Richard, Duke of Gloucester, the region found something of a champion. A national figure, the king's brother no less, who seemed willing to take up the challenge of balancing the scales between north and south a little. Richard petitioned his brother to permit the establishment of a new northern trade organisation in the Low Countries to provide York with the same benefits London was enjoying. Although he was unable to obtain this concession, Edward did issue a proclamation encouraging fairer trade between the regions.

Richard was more successful in dealing with fishgarths in York's rivers. In November 1477, Richard again used his influence over his brother, this time with more success. When the city officials appealed to Richard, he responded by advising them that he had raised the matter with the king who had permitted Richard to 'take a view of oversight of such garths and weirs' and to have them dismantled if they had not been authorised by the justices of eyre. Fishgarths frequently benefitted the more powerful and wealthier sections of society, but Richard showed himself willing to act against these interests.

The administration of equitable law and order is also notable where Richard's hand can be seen, often acting against the established norms of retaining which traditionally caused a lord to protect his retainers against the attentions of the law. Amongst the Parliament Rolls of the sitting opened in 1472 but which continued for a long time to deal with the fallout of the readeption and then the return of Edward IV is a petition on behalf of Katherine Williamson of Howden, near York. Her husband had apparently been ambushed, robbed and killed on the road by three brothers, Robert, Richard and John Farnell. The brothers went to their father Thomas who, 'knowing that all his said sons had committed the aforesaid felonies, murders and robberies' provided shelter to them 'on the same day and on several later occasions'. Thomas then tried to have himself and his sons entered into the service of 'the most high and mighty prince and most honourable lord Richard, duke of Gloucester' so that all four would be 'supported in their horrible felony' by the maintenance of their new lord.

This plan initially worked, with Thomas 'calling himself a servant of the said duke and wearing his clothing, which he had obtained and received by crafty and devious means'. This ended as soon as Richard was notified of the offences Thomas and his sons were accused of when he immediately 'commanded that the said Thomas should be brought to the gaol at York to remain there until he was lawfully acquitted or attainted'. Thomas and his sons had clearly expected to be protected by

Richard as members of his affinity, but they were instead ordered to face the consequences of their actions.

In 1480, John Randson appealed to Richard for help against Sir Robert Claxton of Horden, who Randson claimed was preventing him from working his own land. Claxton was a leading member of the local gentry and also had a son and a son-in-law in Richard's service, an arrangement he might have expected would see him championed and protected. Instead, Richard wrote to Claxton to advise him that he had found in Randson's favour, warning Claxton 'so to demean you that we have no cause to provide his legal remedy in this behalf'. In April 1482, Richard oversaw the trial and punishment of one of his own retainers, Thomas Redhead, for an offence he was accused of committing against a citizen of York.

Richard's apparent willingness to champion the cause of the north of England in ways that were not, at least directly, to his own advantage endeared him to the region. His evident commitment to fair and equitable justice that ignored social standing and the expected norms of the system of livery and maintenance must be part of the reason he became well-loved in the region. The fact that Richard was willing to push against the fabric of society is also crucial in understanding some of the concern about his arrival in London in 1483. It may have contributed to his failure to solidify his position as king, but it has also meant that his memory has remained popular and well-liked in the north, and particularly in Yorkshire, ever since.

Little known fact:

Livery and maintenance was the system of lords providing for their social inferiors in return for their loyalty. Livery referred to the provision of a uniform or a badge denoting the retained man's commitment, and maintenance was the protection the retained man could expect from his lord in return for his loyalty. In the early medieval period, such systems had a root in chivalric brotherhood and responsibility, but by the fifteenth century, it had become corrupted into a way for nobles to show their power and strength in numbers of retainers and for unscrupulous individuals to gain protection from powerful lords. Henry VII would implement rules requiring a royal licence to retain men.

Glossary:

Fishgarths were large-scale networks of fishing nets set up across rivers, in this particular case the Aire, which caught fish such as salmon. They were problematic and unpopular because they hampered river navigation and drastically reduced the catch available downriver for the poorer man.

Did Richard Murder George, Duke of Clarence?

On 12 April 1477, George, Duke of Clarence's men burst into the house of Ankarette Twynyho in Somerset and seized her. Three days later, she was in Warwick and on the morning of the fourth day, she was tried, convicted and sentenced to death for the murder of George's wife, Isabel Neville. She was hanged at Myton the same day. Ankarette had been one of Isabel's ladies in waiting, and George accused her of poisoning his wife, though it seems likely that she died of consumption. George had exercised regal powers of justice that he didn't possess and it was to be the beginning of the end of his long history of disputes with his brother Edward IV.

Shakespeare's Richard, at the beginning of the play bearing his name, speaks to his brother George, who is being transported to the Tower because of a prophecy that 'G' will disinherit Edward's heirs. George is assumed to be the threat, rather than Richard, who is known as Gloucester in the play and is the real 'G' who plans to cause trouble. Richard commiserates with his brother, but after George is taken away, Richard confesses 'Go, tread the path that thou shalt ne'er return. Simple, plain Clarence! I do love thee so, That I will shortly send thy soul to heaven'.

Richard has long been associated with the death of his brother George as a result of Shakespeare's character's admission, but contemporary sources tell a very different, almost polar opposite story. George had been forgiven his betrayal in 1469 when he had joined Warwick to expel Edward. Following the reconciliation in 1471 on Edward's return, George, along with Richard, had negotiated hard for a share of the Neville inheritance. He may have tried to hide Anne Neville away to prevent her marrying at all and forcing him to share the Warwick estates with her husband, but the truth of this episode is not known for certain.

George had been at Edward's side during the signing of the Treaty of Picquigny in France when Richard had refused to attend, yet Isabel's death seemed to reignite something in George. Isabel died on 22 December 1476, and for some reason, George waited until April 1477 to react. His attainder would mention attempts to smuggle his son Edward out of the country to safety before George rebelled and that might explain the delay, but the execution of Ankarette Twynyho was not the end.

When an astronomer called John Stacey, who the *Crowland Chronicle* described as a 'great sorcerer', was arrested for using dark magic, he offered up the name of Thomas Burdet as an accomplice, and both men were hanged, though they went to the gallows protesting their innocence. Burdet had been a member of George's household and the day after the executions, George burst into a Council meeting and denounced the king's justice. George brought with him Dr William Goddard, a Lancastrian by sympathy, who was ordered to read Stacey and Burdet's final speeches out to the Council. Edward was at Windsor at the time, but summoned George and had him arrested and placed in the Tower.

When Parliament opened early in 1478, a bill of attainder was brought against George and Edward himself laid out the charges. There was little by way of a trial, and the intention was always to find George guilty and sentence him to death. George was charged with high treason. Edward had charges read that 'a conspiracy against him, the queen, their son and heir and a great part of the nobility of the land has recently come to his knowledge, which treason is more heinous and unnatural than any previous one because it originates from the king's brother the duke of Clarence, whom the king had always loved and generously rewarded'.

The attainder continued to assert that George 'also said that the king was a bastard, not fit to reign, and made men take oaths of allegiance to him without excepting their loyalty to the king'. George denied all of the charges, but Edward persisted, claiming his brother had kept 'an exemplification under the great seal of an agreement made between him and Queen Margaret promising him the crown if Henry VI's line failed'. During Warwick's rebellion, George had been demoted from the focus of his father-in-law's efforts to the heir of the Lancastrian line if it should fail. The accusation now was that George had kept the official acknowledgement of that agreement, which was all the more dangerous since Henry VI's line had now failed, making George the legal heir to the House of Lancaster.

George was executed on 18 February 1478 in private. A story grew up that he was permitted to choose the method of his execution and elected to be drowned in a barrel of malmsey wine, but the method is not recorded with any certainty. The *Crowland Chronicle* reflected that Edward ordered the execution reluctantly and regretted it, noting that a whispering campaign had been going on for some time, with George's every word reported to Edward and vice versa. The Woodville family of Edward's wife, Elizabeth have long been accused of speeding along George's downfall, if not masterminding it, but no contemporary source even hints at Richard being involved at all. Dominic Mancini would write in 1483 that Richard 'was so overcome with grief for his brother … that he was overheard to say he would one day avenge his brother's death', perhaps applying a degree of hindsight and seeking out a cause for the conflict between Richard and the Woodville family after Edward's death.

The fall of George, Duke of Clarence was brought about by George himself, who seems to have been perennially dissatisfied with his lot. Ultimately, Edward brought charges of high treason against his brother and executed him. There was no suggestion of Richard's involvement at the time, and Shakespeare's dramatic blaming of his villain is simply a fabrication. Whether Richard did hold George's death against Edward, Elizabeth or anyone else is not known, but Richard's involvement in plotting and bringing about the death of his brother George is pure fiction.

Little known fact:

A Tudor portrait of a woman long believed to be Margaret Pole, Countess of Salisbury, the daughter of George, Duke of Clarence, shows her wearing a barrel charm on a bracelet on her right wrist. It remains uncertain whether the portrait is of Margaret, but for centuries the item was believed to be a reference to her father's drowning in a barrel of malmsey wine.

Glossary:

Consumption was the medieval name for tuberculosis, a wasting disease that seemed to consume its victims until they died. The Greeks called the disease 'phthisis', which means consumption.

Chapter 4

The Crisis of 1483

Did Richard and the Woodville Family Really Hate Each Other?

There is a perception that Richard, as Duke of Gloucester, hated his sister-in-law Elizabeth Woodville and all of her family. It is frequently argued that this animosity was the cause of Richard's arrest of Anthony Woodville, Earl Rivers in 1483 and his opposition to the dowager queen on his arrival in London, ultimately culminating in his seizure of the throne. Is there really evidence of a long-running feud between the king's brother and his wife's family?

Much of the weight for the idea of a feud comes from Dominic Mancini, an Italian visitor to London during the spring of 1483. As an eyewitness, his testimony is given a great deal of weight, but there are significant problems with this source, not least the current translation from the Latin that is widely used. Mancini spoke no English and demonstrates a lack of understanding of English politics so that some of the wider information he provides is not accurate. Nevertheless, Mancini explains that Richard's hatred of the queen's family stemmed from the execution of his older brother George, Duke of Clarence in 1478.

Mancini notes that Elizabeth Woodville became terrified of George and 'concluded that her offspring by the king would never come to the throne, unless the duke of Clarence were removed'. This fear led to George's prosecution and execution for treason, as a direct result of which Mancini suggests 'Richard duke of Gloucester was so overcome with grief for his brother, that he could not dissimulate so well, but that he was overheard to say that he would one day avenge his brother's death.' This sets up the bitter rivalry that would be played out in London in 1483, but is there any real evidence for what Mancini alleges?

The Woodville family had risen quickly, firstly with Elizabeth's father's marriage to the widowed Jacquetta, Duchess of Bedford and then with her own union with Edward IV. Elizabeth's father, Richard Woodville, had been created Earl Rivers but had been killed, along with one of his sons, by the Earl of Warwick during his uprising in 1469. Elizabeth was the oldest of thirteen children who survived to adulthood. Anthony was the second child and as the oldest son became Earl Rivers on his father's death. Although initially a Lancastrian family, the Woodvilles became firmly tied to the Yorkist cause with Elizabeth's marriage to the king.

A feud between Edward IV's closest friend, Lord Hastings, and at least some of the Woodville family, particularly Elizabeth Woodville's oldest son from her first marriage, Thomas Grey, Marquis of Dorset is well attested to. It apparently lay behind some of the events in the aftermath of Edward's death, but there is remarkably little to suggest that such tension existed with Richard. There is no evidence that Richard hated his sister-in-law, though his mother, Cecily Neville, Duchess of York appears to have taken umbrage at the low match her oldest son had made for himself. It is, therefore, possible that either Richard possessed some of the same prejudices or that his mother's opinion swayed his own, yet Richard maintained a good enough relationship with his brother to suggest that there was nothing as strong as hatred.

Anthony Woodville and Richard, Duke of Gloucester were very similar characters in many ways. Anthony was known as a soldier and a scholar. He had his own translation of *The Dictes and Sayings of the Philosophers* printed by William Caxton in 1477, making him an early patron of the printing press that was about to revolutionise Europe. Richard was also interested in this new technology and owned an extensive library. Both men enjoyed a solid reputation as soldiers, Anthony also becoming the most famed Englishman at tournaments, a pursuit Richard does not appear to have participated in. Just as Richard was placed in charge of the northern regions of Edward's kingdom, Anthony was given control of the young Prince of Wales and his household, allowing him to exercise a great deal of authority in Wales.

Richard would arrest Anthony on their way to London and send him north, where he would later be executed. When Anthony sat to write his final will and testament on 23 June 1483, it is perhaps telling that he appointed several men close to Richard as executors. He also wrote 'Over this, I besech humbly, my Lord of Gloucestyr, in the worshipp of Cristes passhion and for the meryte and wele of his sowle, to comfort help and assist, as supervisor (for very trust) of this testament, that myn executours may with his pleasure fulfill this my last will.' Anthony chose to appoint Richard as supervisor of his executors, which at least suggests a degree of trust. It is hard to tell whether Anthony was merely recognising that Richard was now in power or whether it was something of an admission of guilt in the accusations of a Woodville plot against Richard.

It is hard to establish the true nature of the relation between Richard and his sister-in-law's family. There is no real evidence, beyond anecdotal opinions like that of the poorly briefed Mancini, that they despised each other. Richard and Anthony Woodville had similar high reputations and rarely had cause to operate in the same political spheres in a way that might breed vendettas. There is no evidence that Richard disliked Edward's wife either, beyond the possibility of sharing his mother's opinion, of which there is no evidence. After Easter 1484, Elizabeth came to terms with Richard as king and allowed her daughters to enter their uncle's protection, suggesting again that there was no long-term hatred between the two. It remains impossible to prove whether the two sides really hated each other, but neither is there any evidence of a running feud. Trying to see problems in the relationships between Richard and the Woodvilles is perhaps the application of hindsight. When Anthony Woodville went to Northampton to meet Richard, he appears to have gone in good faith, something that doesn't seem to have changed as he wrote his will after Richard had arrested him.

Little known fact:

Anthony Woodville was one of the most famous tournament knights in Europe, something that distinguishes him from Richard. As far as we know, there is no record of Richard ever taking part in a joust or a tournament, perhaps because of the problems caused by his scoliosis. Anthony took part in a huge and famous match with the Bastard of Burgundy, an illegitimate son of the Duke of Burgundy, in 1466.

Did Richard Kidnap Edward V at Stony Stratford?

King Edward IV died on 9 April 1483 at Westminster. He was nineteen days short of his forty-first birthday and had been king for twenty-two years, with the exception of about six months during the readeption. Vigorous and athletic in his youth, Edward had put on weight and spent his time in pleasure during his later years. He holds the impressive records of never having lost a battle in his life – no mean feat during the Wars of the Roses. Edward reportedly picked up a chill while fishing and after a brief illness, he died, and the unexpected nature of his removal from the political scene created huge problems.

The first issue was that Edward's son and heir, now proclaimed King Edward V, was only twelve years old and was at Ludlow, still undergoing the training his father had designed to prepare him to become king. Such a young king was always problematical as they were not deemed able to rule in their own right, leading almost inevitably to power struggles, the potential for abuse of that power and a failure to adequately prepare the boy for government. Richard II had come to the throne in 1377 at the age of ten and been deposed in 1399 after descending into tyranny. Even more recently, Henry VI had become king in 1422 aged just nine months, been unseated in 1461 and his rule had been disastrous for England. The country was likely to be made nervous by the accession of a minor, particularly so close to the dynastic struggles that had disrupted the nation.

A second problem existed that was to influence the events that followed. Edward IV had a personality to match his frame and everyone liked him. Effusive commentators noted that he made even the most common man feel at ease in his presence and that he could recall the names of everyone he ever met should he see them again. For years, Edward had been the glue that kept members of his court together around him at the centre. He was able to restrain factional infighting in a way that Henry VI had fatally failed to do, and an impending minority caused the lid to blow off these rivalries. The most significant dispute in London was between the Woodville family of Edward's wife, the dowager queen Elizabeth and William, Lord Hastings, Edward's closest friend. In particular, Hastings and Thomas Grey, Edward IV's stepson, maintained a deep rivalry and hatred of each other.

A plaque on a building on the high street of Stony Stratford. There is no real evidence of where Edward V lodged, and the confident assertion of his subsequent murder is typical of the myth making that surrounds Richard III's story and reputation. (Author's collection)

Richard had spent most of the last decade or so in the north of England, away from the power politics of London. It is believed that Elizabeth Woodville did not write to advise Richard of his brother's death. Instead Lord Hastings sent word, urging Richard to come south quickly because the Woodvilles were planning to snatch power and exclude Richard, who had been appointed Lord Protector in a codicil added to Edward's will shortly before his death. There is no record of the communications that took place, but this version of events seems to have become accepted. If it is true, it makes it essential to understand that Richard left the north already wary of plots and threats that he might encounter when he reached London. The late addition to Edward's will also strongly suggests that he was aware of what might happen after he died and saw Richard as the perfect foil to the feuding.

It is believed, though again there is no surviving evidence to prove the arrangement, that Richard organised with Anthony Woodville, Earl

Rivers, who was the head of Edward V's household at Ludlow and who was responsible for his education and upbringing, to meet at Northampton and travel on to London together. The new king left Ludlow on 24 April, Anthony Woodville having waited to celebrate St George's Day on 23 April before departing. Edward's coronation was being arranged for just ten days later on 4 May, and it is believed that Richard was to meet the new king's party at Northampton on 29 April.

Edward V's party arrived in Northampton first, but travelled on some fifteen miles to Stony Stratford, just past the Woodville manor of Grafton Regis and in their heartland. Anthony Woodville remained behind to meet Richard at Northampton. When his party arrived from the north, it would not be unreasonable for Richard to have been put further on edge by the news that Edward was no longer in Northampton and had travelled onwards. Precisely what happened that night is unknown, but in the morning, Richard moved swiftly to arrest Anthony Woodville and ride to Stony Stratford where he also seized Thomas Vaughan, Edward's Chamberlain, and Sir Richard Grey, the new king's step-brother, younger brother to Thomas Grey. Richard had these men sent north and took Edward into his own custody before continuing, slowly, to London, arriving on 4 May, the date tentatively set for the coronation.

The incident at Stony Stratford and the arrest of key figures around Edward V are traditionally seen as a ruthless signal of Richard's intention to seize the throne. Tudor historian Polydore Vergil pinpoints the night spent at Northampton as the moment that Richard tells his ally Henry Stafford, Duke of Buckingham that he is planning to take the throne. It is certain that the removal of those who had been closest to the young boy as he grew up must have been unsettling for the new king amidst all the other upheaval. He would barely have known his uncle Richard, particularly compared to his uncle Anthony.

Nevertheless, it is perhaps not unreasonable that Richard acted out of caution. If Hastings had warned him of Woodville plotting, if Richard was aware of the factions breaking out in London and if he saw his responsibility at that point as being to ensure his nephew's safe succession for the sake of his brother's memory and for the House of York more generally, then taking potential threats into custody is perhaps not unreasonable. As the king's paternal uncle and the senior adult male of the royal house, Richard caused no real concern by taking control of the king. When they arrived in London, they were warmly welcomed, and the Council would praise Richard's actions. That wasn't to be the end of the story, though.

Little known fact:

Edward IV is the tallest monarch ever to rule England or Britain. He was 6'4", 2 inches taller than his grandson Henry VIII and an inch taller than Prince William, so he looks likely to hold his record for a while yet. Richard's skeleton shows that he would have stood at 5'8" tall, but the curvature of his spine due to scoliosis meant that he, in fact, appeared several inches shorter.

Richard Definitely Murdered Lord Hastings, Didn't He?

William, Lord Hastings was a cornerstone of Edward IV's government. He had been a close friend to the king from the beginning of his reign and had grown wealthy and powerful through the service he had given. During the months in exile, Hastings had joined Edward and Richard, and after their return, he had continued to reap the rewards his loyalty brought. According to the traditional version of the muddled events of 1483, it was Hastings who informed Richard of his brother's death and warned him of a Woodville plot, advising him to hurry south. Just over a month after Richard arrived in London, he ordered Hastings' execution in an act viewed, even by those sympathetic to Richard, as unforgivable and inexplicable. Is this an indefensible act of murder?

The position of Lord Protector is a peculiarly English, peculiarly fifteenth-century, creation. The codicil to Edward IV's will appointing Richard to this post has not survived, but he was confirmed in the office at a meeting of Council on 10 May, at least suggesting that it had been his brother's wish. The Protector had responsibility for military matters, both domestic and foreign. The purpose of the role was to protect the kingdom during a minority or the incapacity of a king. It gave Richard no power in government or authority over the king's person, though the Protector would usually be afforded a prominent place at Council too. The office of Lord Protector and a position in government, though, are not the positions that influence an understanding of the events of the Council meeting of 13 June 1483.

Richard had been Lord High Constable of England since October 1469. Except for the readeption period, Richard had held the office for almost fourteen years, from the age of seventeen. When Council met on 13 June, it did so in two locations. The majority met elsewhere, but Richard, Buckingham, Lord Hastings, Bishop Morton and Bishop Rotherham met at the Tower, nominally to conclude arrangements for Edward V's coronation. Thomas More's dramatisation has Richard enter the meeting, leave on a pretence and return crying treason. In the scuffle that follows as guards burst into the room, Lord Hastings is arrested, dragged outside and beheaded.

The key feature of the story is the cry of treason. The powers of the Constable, as defined by Edward IV, permitted the trial of cases of treason based on evidence the Constable has seen. The Constable had authority to act as judge, jury and executioner and there was no right of appeal. It was a profoundly inequitable and unjust process but deemed necessary in the dangerous, fast-moving politics of the Wars of the Roses. Richard had spent his entire adult life in possession of these powers and would have understood what they allowed him to do.

Even later Tudor sources seem to allow that Lord Hastings was up to something. Polydore Vergil wrote that before Richard's arrival in London, Hastings 'called together unto Paul's church such friends as he knew to be right careful for the life, dignity, and estate of prince Edward, and conferred with them what best was to be done'. Grafton recorded that 'Lord Stanley sent to him [Hastings] a trusty and secret messenger at midnight in all the haste, requiring him to rise and ride away with him'. Even Thomas More stated that Richard was informed by a lawyer in Hasting's service, William Catesby, that Lord Hastings was conspiring against the Protector. More wrote that 'Catesby's account of the Lord Hastings's words and discourse, which he so represented to him, as if he had wished and contrived his death' influenced Richard.

No real evidence survives to help decide whether Hastings was genuinely plotting against Richard. It is possible that Hastings began to fear for Edward V's prospects, or that he was making his own bid for

The Manticore badge of William, Lord Hastings, the close friend of Edward IV who was executed at the Tower of London on 13 June 1483 on Richard's orders. (Courtesy of Wikimedia Commons)

power, hoping to use Richard to defeat his Woodville enemies and then his own understanding of and connections within London to remove Richard and make himself the senior figure in government. Understanding this incident will always be coloured by a personal perspective of Richard and the events of that spring. Grafton later wrote that Richard showed his evidence to the aldermen of London immediately after the execution and that they were satisfied 'that the Lord Hastings and other of his conspiracy had contrived to have suddenly destroyed him and the Duke of Buckingham there the same day in council'.

What Richard did on 13 June 1483 was effectively to convene a Court of Chivalry under the Constable at which Lord Hastings was tried for treason, based on evidence Richard had seen, found guilty with no right of appeal and summarily executed. It is a process that doubtless sounds unpalatable to modern ears, but was nevertheless a legal framework within which Richard was entitled to operate. The morality of this action remains open to question and will rest upon a personal belief either in Richard's fabrication of evidence to facilitate Hasting's downfall or in the genuine conviction that Hastings was conspiring against Richard as Protector. Whether the evidence was real or not, the technical legality of his execution of Lord Hastings is not open to dispute. As Lord High Constable of England, Richard acted within powers that his brother had given to him fourteen years earlier. Lord Hastings was judicially executed, not murdered. The question is whether he used those powers to protect himself and his nephew from a perceived threat or to eliminate opposition to a planned coup.

Little known fact:

The Lord High Constable was one of the nine Great Offices of State in medieval England, ranking seventh in order of precedence, below the Lord Great Chamberlain but above the Earl Marshal. These Great Offices formed the basis of medieval government in England and several, including the Lord High Admiral (a position Richard also held) and Lord High Chancellor, are still in use today.

Did Richard Murder Anthony Woodville, Sir Richard Grey and Thomas Vaughan?

On 25 June 1483, Anthony Woodville, Earl Rivers, the brother of the dowager queen Elizabeth Woodville and uncle to the new King Edward V, was executed at Pontefract Castle in Yorkshire. Sir Richard Grey, the younger of Elizabeth Woodville's sons from her first marriage, and Thomas Vaughan, who had been Chamberlain to Edward V in Ludlow, were also executed. These deaths, like that of Lord Hastings, are often viewed as stepping stones on Richard's path to the throne, obstacles that he had to remove to attain what many hold to be his long-term ambition.

These three deaths are also frequently equated with that of Hastings in terms of their questionable legality and morality. When Council met on 10 May, the meeting at which Richard was formally appointed Lord

Protector, it is also recorded that Richard attempted to have Rivers, Grey and Vaughan accused of treason, but his request was refused by Council. Richard, a relative stranger to London's political scene, might have become concerned at the meaning and implications of this. If Woodville support remained strong in Council, he might have considered himself to still be at risk from that faction.

The legal explanation for Richard's actions may well lie in precisely the same powers as Constable of England that made Lord Hastings' execution legal. Simultaneously, this reliance highlights the fact that Richard planned to make this move before the order was sent. The Constable was able to appoint a deputy, who in turn could convene a Court of Chivalry and prosecute cases of treason using the same powers as the Constable. When River, Grey and Vaughan were arrested at Stony Stratford, Richard might have tried them there and then using those same powers if their swift elimination had been his priority. Instead, he

The remains of the Banqueting Hall at Sudeley Castle, Gloucestershire, built during Richard's ownership of the property. (Author's collection)

Plaster impressions of the Great Seal used by Richard III, located at St Akelda's Church, Middleham, at which Richard attended services.

sent them north: Rivers to Sheriff Hutton Castle, Grey to Middleham Castle and Vaughan to Pontefract Castle. These were key properties in Richard's portfolio, and the use of three separate destinations is an important feature.

Historian Annette Carson has suggested that Richard intended to use these men as hostages to force the dowager queen to come to terms with him. This is a viable proposal since Richard might have executed them all on the spot at Stony Stratford. If that had been his plan, he must have realised within a short time of arriving in London that it was not working. Elizabeth Woodville remained in sanctuary with her daughters, Edward IV's youngest son and her own oldest, Thomas Grey. Richard attempted to have the men accused of treason as early as 10 May but to no avail. Being restrained by the Council might have been an uncomfortable novelty for Richard after his free rein in the north.

If Rivers, Grey and Vaughan did receive a trial under the auspices of the Court of Chivalry, it is possible to piece together the necessary parts. On 10 June, Richard wrote to the city of York asking them to send men 'to aid and assist us against the Queen, her blood adherents and affinity' who he claimed were plotting to kill him, Buckingham and the 'old royal blood of this realm'. The following day, he sent further letters to the Earl of Northumberland, Baron Neville and others ordering a muster at Pontefract on 18 June. Northumberland, the most senior member of the nobility left in the north, would have been a perfect selection to act as a deputy to the Constable. If the intention were simply to illegally murder the three men, it would be odd and unnecessary to go to the trouble of gathering them all at Pontefract from their different locations.

It is, therefore, possible that Richard appointed Northumberland as his deputy Constable, instructing him to convene a Court of Chivalry. Rous refers to Northumberland acting as their 'judge'. If so, Rivers, Grey and Vaughan were brought to Pontefract for what constituted, legally at least, a trial and execution. If this was not the case, the focus of attention on Pontefract and the moving of two of the three prisoners from other castles to that location do not make sense. By the time of the executions on 25 June, it also meant that Richard had been planning this course of action for a fortnight.

The traditional interpretation of these executions as being part of a plot to remove Edward V's support and thereby clear Richard's path to the throne should not be ignored. In the absence of conclusive evidence, it remains as plausible an explanation as that involving a legal trial. Indeed, the two need not be mutually exclusive. Motive may not be relevant to the method, since Richard might have cleared his path using legal mechanisms at his disposal and without, technically, breaking the law.

Eliminating Hastings and Rivers might also have been viewed by Richard as a requirement of his position and perhaps even as his brother's intention. Edward appointed his brother because he was all too aware of the factions at court that would erupt on his death and threaten his son. Before arriving in London, Richard had reportedly been warned of the Woodville faction's intentions, his wariness perhaps heightened by their failure to meet him with the new king at the location arranged. In the capital, Hastings has been reported as holding meetings against Richard, and it appears one of his lawyers, William Catesby, informed Richard that Hastings was plotting his death. As the cauldron of infighting his brother had feared reached boiling point, Richard might have decided that removing the heads – literally and figuratively – from the two sides was the best way to restore order, enforce his will and protect his nephew.

As with the death of Lord Hastings, Richard motives and intentions remain questionable, but it seems likely that the executions of Rivers, Grey and Vaughan had a legal basis.

Little known fact:

It has been reported that the bodies of Rivers, Grey and Vaughan were thrown into unmarked graves after their execution, but Vaughan's remains would end up at Westminster Abbey. Either they were retrieved after 1485 or the rumour is untrue and the bodies were more honourably treated.

Was There A Pre-Contract That Made Edward IV's Children Illegitimate?

The declaration of the illegitimacy of Edward IV's children based on his bigamy is one of the most important and divisive issues in the web of events of June 1483. It impacts a perception of Richard's motives and the nature of his intentions, though it tells us little about how early those plans may have developed. The question of whether a pre-contract really existed is a key one, but evidence remains sparse and inconclusive. So how close can we get to establishing whether there really was a pre-contract that would make Edward IV and Elizabeth Woodville's marriage illegal and their children illegitimate?

The notion of a pre-contract to marry is perhaps unfamiliar to modern ears. It is an area of canon law that is no longer in use but which was entirely legal and enforceable during the medieval period. A contract to marry could be created easily and quite informally by a promise to marry someone. 'I will marry you' was enough to create a contract and in the eyes of the law, that was equivalent to a full marriage, particularly if the relationship was consummated afterwards. If the pre-contract were real, then Edward's marriage to Elizabeth Woodville was bigamous, and their children were technically illegitimate and therefore unable to inherit the throne.

King Edward IV, Richard's oldest brother. (Courtesy of Yale Center For British Art, Paul Mellon Collection)

The romantic image of the Princes in the Tower as innocent children murdered on the orders of their uncle, Richard III. (Courtesy of Yale Center For British Art, Paul Mellon Fund)

The precise nature of the accusation is not entirely clear from the sources. Dominic Mancini, an Italian writer who was in London during these events, provides an eyewitness account, though he spoke no English and was, therefore, relying on information from others. Mancini recorded that a sermon was preached claiming that 'Edward, they say, was conceived in adultery and in every way was unlike the late duke of York, whose son he was falsely said to be, but Richard, duke of Gloucester, who altogether resembled his father, was to come to the throne as the legitimate successor'. This version of the sermon describes Edward IV's own illegitimacy in what would have been a brutal attack on the reputation of Richard's own mother. Polydore Vergil, writing in the next century, noted that Cecily Neville, Richard's mother, complained 'in sundry places to right many noble men' of the offence her son caused.

The *Crowland Chronicle*, the section covering these events compiled in 1486 by an unknown but politically well-informed writer, tells a different version of this tale. 'It was set forth, by way of prayer, in an address in a certain roll of parchment, that the sons of king Edward were bastards, on the ground that he had contracted a marriage with one lady Eleanor Boteler, before his marriage to queen Elizabeth'. Crowland makes no mention of an accusation about Edward's own illegitimacy and instead refers to a pre-contract to marry Lady Eleanor Butler. This lady was a daughter of John Talbot, Earl of Shrewsbury, who later married Sir Thomas Butler.

Philippe de Commynes, a Burgundian who later entered the service of the King of France, recorded in his memoirs that Robert Stillington, Bishop of Bath and Wells came to Richard in early June and revealed the pre-contract, providing evidence of the service at which he had officiated. This evidence has not survived, but it was reportedly presented to those who had gathered in London in preparation for a Parliament. It is essential to understand that Parliament was not in session at this time, though. Whatever evidence was shown appears to have convinced those who saw it because Edward IV's children were declared illegitimate and Richard was petitioned to take the throne. It is possible that any evidence was destroyed after 1485 when Henry VII needed to ensure his intended bride, Edward IV's oldest daughter Elizabeth of York, was re-legitimised.

Edward's reputation may have been a key element of his son's downfall at this point. Commynes, who had met Edward during his exile in Burgundy, noted that 'His thoughts were wholly employed upon the ladies (and far more than was reasonable)'. Amongst the three reasons Commynes gives for Edward being readily accepted back into London after his exile in 1471 is another reference to his reputation with the ladies. Commynes believed that the wives of London encouraged their husbands to support Edward's return because they hoped for a swift return to his bed and the favour that brought. If a carnal reputation served Edward well in 1471, it was to be the undoing of his son in 1483. The charge of agreeing to a pre-contract in order to get a young lady into bed may well have felt plausible to those who knew Edward. A secret marriage was also not beyond the realms of possibility since his marriage to Elizabeth Woodville had been conducted in secret and kept from the Council for several months.

The charge that the timing of the revelations by Stillington was too convenient for Richard is frequently used to add weight to the notion that the story was a fabrication to justify seizing the throne, but it is unlikely that Stillington would have revealed such damning evidence during Edward IV's lifetime. The bishop had been imprisoned when George, Duke of Clarence had fallen and would be again immediately after Henry VII took the throne. Had he revealed what he knew earlier, it would surely have cost him his life. Perhaps the old man had hoped to die before the accession of one he knew to be illegitimate, but Edward's early death and the impending coronation forced his hand. If that is the case, it was anything but convenient for Richard as he tried to quell the bickering factions and arrange his nephew's coronation.

The existence of a pre-contract to marry between Edward IV and Eleanor Butler cannot be proven. There is evidence to suggest that it was sufficiently established in 1483 for men of authority to act on what they had seen, but the distorting of the stories of the sermon's content and possible later destruction of evidence make it impossible to say for certain that a pre-contract made Edward IV's children illegitimate. However, it cannot be entirely disproven, either.

Little known fact:

Sir Thomas More, whose veracity as a source is frequently relied on in matters relating to Richard, wrote that Edward IV had been pre-contracted to marry a lady named Dame Elizabeth Lucy, not Lady Eleanor Butler. Was this a deliberate mistake to stop anyone trying to find the truth about the pre-contract when evidence might still have existed, or a genuine error? Either way, it makes More's evidence suspect.

Chapter 5

Taking The Throne

Did Richard III Usurp the Throne in 1483?

The nature of Richard's ascent to the throne in June 1483 remains one of the most contentious and hotly debated issues amongst the events of his life. Consistently referred to as a usurpation of his young nephew's throne, the use of the term 'usurp' is almost as frequently challenged. Dominic Mancini's *De Ocupatione* has been translated as 'The Usurpation' rather than 'The Occupation', which it literally means, to fit this traditional narrative. Understanding the nature of usurpation and the application of the word, in this case, requires the stripping away of emotive language and a shift to a more legal argument.

It is perhaps unhelpful to this situation that the word 'usurp' has different definitions. The entry available at oxforddictionaries.com defines 'usurp' as 'Take (a position of power or importance) illegally or by force.' Richard did not come to power by an armed coup, nor was there any battle involved in a dispute over the throne. The legality is a more opaque matter. It is important to separate the legal aspects of Richard claim to the throne from the more emotive questions of whether the charges of illegitimacy against the children of Edward IV were true or not.

Identifying the legal mechanism responsible for appointing a king is difficult in medieval England. It is true that traditionally, the oldest surviving son of a reigning monarch was considered his heir and the next legal king, but Parliament had been acquiring an increasing role in legitimising a king's claim, particularly during the upheavals of the second half of the fifteenth century. Before the Norman Conquest, Anglo-Saxon kings were appointed and approved by the Witan, a council of leading nobles and churchmen and it was by no means certain that a king's oldest son would follow him. Immediately after the Norman Conquest, William the Conqueror left England to his second son, William Rufus, giving the Duchy of Normandy to his oldest son Robert.

During the Norman and Angevin period, there was technically a break between the death of the old king and the proclamation of a new ruler during which government legally ceased. This situation was only remedied at the end of Henry III's reign (died 1272) when his son, Edward I was on crusade. Before Edward left, Henry provided for authority to pass to Edward immediately on his death, without the need for a proclamation or a coronation to confirm the succession.

The succession became an issue once more as Edward III outlived his oldest son, Edward, the Black Prince. The crown passed to the Black Prince's young son, Richard II, who was, in turn, deposed by Henry IV in 1399. Henry IV was approved in removing Richard II by the majority of the nobility, and that appears to have been considered sufficient to cause Richard II to abdicate in favour of his cousin. The third Lancastrian king, Henry VI, was deposed in 1461 by Edward IV, who was petitioned at Baynard's Castle in London by those nobles in the city along with the aldermen. His title was then presented to Parliament for approval after the crushing victory at the Battle of Towton. The Yorkist period saw Parliament reach a new pinnacle as the ultimate arbiter of royal titles. In 1460, it had debated the merits of Henry VI's claim against that of Richard, Duke of York and in 1461, it approved the accession of his heir as Edward IV.

When Richard was offered the crown in 1483, it was done in a method almost identical to Edward's ascent in 1461. Richard was also at Baynards Castle when a delegation of officials petitioned him to take the throne and Parliament would also outline and effectively approve his title when it sat in 1484. Perhaps the significant difference is the absence of a battle before Richard's coronation. The definition of usurpation that requires an illegal assumption of power or the use of force to achieve it is difficult to apply to Richard's circumstances. The legality depends on a view taken of the process of being petitioned to take the throne, accepting and then having Parliament ratify the title. Although this does not follow any statute, it at least appears to have been an accepted, legal form of removing one monarch and appointing another.

Some dictionaries apply a different, looser definition of 'usurp', For example, the Collins English Dictionary defines it as 'seize (a position or power) without authority'. The difficulty with this definition is that it again requires a test of the authority used to depose Edward V and place Richard III on the throne. The argument is not dissimilar to that about illegality, in that it requires a definition of where the authority to appoint or approve title to the crown lies. It appears to have rested with Parliament to some degree by this point and Parliament was not in session when Richard was petitioned to take the throne, though the request was made by men who would have sat in Parliament had it been open. The fait accompli was then ratified by Parliament in 1484.

It is odd that Richard is so frequently singled out as a usurper amidst other monarchs who might be deemed to have taken the throne in similarly dubious circumstances. Of the eighteen monarchs from William the Conqueror to Richard III many might be accused of being usurpers if Richard was. William I took the crown by conquest, Henry I overrode the better claim of his older brother, Stephen took the crown from his cousin Matilda, who had been recognised as heir. Henry II became king after the civil war known as The Anarchy and his son John took the throne despite a pre-eminent claim resting in his nephew, Arthur. Henry IV deposed Richard II, and Edward IV unseated Henry VI, who was in turn restored by force. If Richard was a usurper, then it was far from a singular event, and he would lose his throne to Henry Tudor in a manner that fits the definitions far more clearly. The fact remains that even this charge is unproven against Richard by most definitions of the word.

Little known fact:

Henry VII initially dated his reign from the day before the Battle of Bosworth so that he could convict those who had fought for Richard III of treason. Henry was later forced to undo this when he discovered men were unwilling to take the field for him when they might be similarly accused of treason if he lost.

Did Richard III Kill The Princes in the Tower?

One of the greatest mysteries still unresolved in all of history is the fate of the sons of Edward IV. Edward V and Richard of Shrewsbury, Duke of York are remembered as the Princes in the Tower and have long been

The White Tower of the Tower of London. Edward V and his younger brother Richard, Duke of York, remembered as the Princes in the Tower, were lodged at the Tower to prepare for Edward's coronation and it is believed they were later moved into the White Tower, after which there were no more recorded sightings of them. (Author's collection)

assumed to have been murdered by their uncle on his ruthless path to become King Richard III. As with all things during 1483, it is not quite that simple, and this murder mystery defies resolution over 500 years later – if there was even a murder at all.

Cold, hard facts remain sparse. The last date set for Edward V's coronation was 22 June. Instead, a sermon was preached on that day espousing the illegitimacy of him and his siblings. Richard was petitioned to take the throne and a coronation date set at 6 July. Edward and his brother had been occupying the royal apartments in the Tower of London as was traditional for monarchs preparing for a coronation. Since these rooms were now required for Richard and Anne, the boys were moved, possibly into the Garden Tower near the curtain wall, though this is not certain. There are poorly documented rumours of an attempt to break the boys out of the Tower soon after Richard's coronation, which is believed to have led to them being moved again, probably, but not certainly, into

David Garrick in the role of Shakespeare's King Richard III, the enduring image of the king in the public consciousness. (Courtesy of Yale Center For British Art)

the White Tower at the centre of the Tower of London complex. They began to be seen less and less until reports of them ceased. There is no date of their last sighting but was possibly as late as early September. After that, they disappear entirely from the record.

Richard III has long been the prime suspect and has stood convicted in the court of public opinion. The most persuasive hostile witness is William Shakespeare who not only wrote drama rather than fact but who may have used Richard as a convenient cover to write about the politics of his own day, in particular about Robert Cecil. Writers at the beginning of the sixteenth century, including Sir Thomas More and Polydore Vergil, wrote of Richard ordering the murders and Sir James Tyrell carrying out the evil deed. Polydore Vergil, who had been engaged by Henry VII to write a history of England, also reported rumours that the boys had not been killed. He noted that 'It was generally reported and believed that the sons of Edward IV were still alive, having been conveyed secretly away and obscurely concealed in some distant region.' Even official Tudor sources were not entirely sure about what had happened.

A traditional murder investigation, looking for motive, means and opportunity, would surely treat Richard as the prime suspect. His nephews were in his care when they disappeared, and if they were the focus of attempts to free them and place Edward V back on the throne, then the motive would be a desperate bid for self-preservation. The most significant single issue with believing that Richard ordered the boys' deaths is that if he did so, it was to prevent them from being a threat. To make such a threat end, the death of both boys would need to be widely publicised. Richard could blame a plague or other illness of some kind, a betrayal or assassin within the Tower or claim their deaths had been caused by a botched attempt to free them. It didn't need to be convincing, but everyone needed to know that Edward IV's sons were dead. Murdering them and keeping it quiet achieved nothing. They could still be a threat, as Henry VII would discover.

It remains possible that the Princes in the Tower were never murdered. They might have been snatched away by adherents of their father or mother, or Richard may simply have moved them into his northern estates, surrounded by men he knew and trusted until he was secure enough for them to re-emerge. There is a precedent for such a thing. When Henry IV took the throne from Richard II in 1399, he overlooked Richard's heirs presumptive, the eight-year-old Edmund Mortimer and his younger brother Roger. Although the Mortimer claim was in the female line from Edward III, it was considered by many to be better than the Lancastrian male line claim of Henry. Edmund and Roger were placed in Berkeley Castle and closely watched. A few years into Henry IV's reign, the boys were abducted, and an attempt made to deliver them to Owain Glyndwr, who was leading a rebellion in Wales, with the intention of making Edmund king. The brothers were recovered before they reached Glyndwr and then vanished for many years, kept under much closer supervision. On Henry V's accession in 1413, they were released, and Edmund was permitted to take up the family lands and titles as Earl of March. Roger died shortly after their release and Edmund passed away in 1425. Their fates may have offered a template for

NORTHCOTE.

NO. III.

The Disposal of the Princes in the Tower, showing an imagined scene of the bodies of Edward V and Richard, Duke of York being taken from the Tower of London after their murders. (Courtesy of Wikimedia Commons)

the passing over of minor heirs. The problem had been their initial loose supervision, which led to them becoming the focus of a plot. After that, they were more securely kept. Might Richard have looked for lessons in their story?

The fate of the sons of Edward IV remains as much a mystery now as it was at the end of the fifteenth century. The bones resting within a marble urn in Westminster Abbey are unlikely to be those of the princes in my opinion. The examination of them in 1933 set out to prove that they were the bones of the two boys rather than objectively trying to establish their origins. If they were murdered in 1483, Richard III must remain the prime suspect, though it would be hard to convict him beyond a reasonable doubt on the available evidence. The boys may have survived, but that cannot be proven either. This point seems likely to remain a hotly debated mystery for some time yet.

Little known fact:

A Tyrell family legend (of the kind that can never be verified) states that Sir James Tyrell entertained Elizabeth Woodville and her daughters at his home, Gipping Hall, when she met with her sons, the Princes in the Tower, during Richard III's reign. If true, this association might be the basis of Tyrell's later alleged involvement in their murder.

Was Buckingham's Rebellion A Serious Threat?

Henry Stafford, Duke of Buckingham had been a key figure in Richard III's ascent to the throne in 1483. He had been in the political wilderness during Edward IV's reign for reasons that are unclear, though which may have been vindicated before the tumultuous year was out. The first serious threat to Richard III's crown came in October 1483, just three months after his coronation, and it has been remembered as Buckingham's Rebellion; but how dangerous was it, why did Buckingham become involved and how did the revolt take his name?

Although it has gone down in history as a monumental failure, it is important to appreciate that at the time, this revolt was on a large scale, was well organised and stood an excellent chance of success. A new regime will always seek to shrug of rebellions as little more than a nuisance, but

Henry Stafford, Duke of Buckingham, largely ignored during Edward IV's reign, he quickly became Richard's closest ally in 1483, only to turn against him and rebel in October. (Courtesy of Yale Center For British Art Yale University Art Gallery Collection)

Richard's reign could easily have ended in October 1483. The date of the uprising was to be 18 October, St Luke's Day. In a highly religious age, people may have been more familiar with saints' days than calendar dates so it may have been easier to spread the word that the Feast of St Luke was the day to launch the rebellion. Kent was to rise first, attacking London from the south-east. With Richard distracted, Wiltshire and Berkshire would rise, aided by Buckingham's men coming from his home at Brecon in Wales to attack Richard's rear. Henry Tudor was also due to land on the south coast, probably in Devon, with an army of Breton mercenaries.

Fortune seemed to favour Richard when the men of Kent sprang into action too early. On 10 October, eight days before St Luke's Day, they marched on London, but John Howard, Duke of Norfolk was in the city and captured several rebels, driving the rest away. When questioned, these men divulged the rest of the plan and Norfolk sent word to Richard, who was in Lincoln, of the threat. Richard called a muster at Leicester and ordered the destruction of bridges over the River Severn to prevent Buckingham crossing. By 18 October, as the rest of the rebels began to move, unaware that their plot had been uncovered and that they were expected, the weather now seemed to favour the new king too. Storms hampered the rebels' progress. The River Severn was a swollen torrent that Buckingham couldn't cross in the absence of bridges and in the Channel, Henry Tudor's fleet was scattered.

From Lincoln, Richard wrote to his Lord Chancellor, Bishop Russell, requesting that he send the Great Seal to the king and the letter has additions in Richard's own hand that demonstrate his rage at Buckingham's betrayal. He wrote of his outrage at 'the malysse of hym that hadde best cawse to be trewe, th'Duc of Bokyngham, the most untrewe creatur lyvyng', adding that 'We assure you ther was never false traytor better purvayde for'. When the rebellion failed, Buckingham went into hiding but was eventually betrayed and handed over. Although he reportedly pleaded for an audience with Richard, he was denied a meeting and executed at Salisbury on 2 November 1483. Henry Tudor's ship came within sight of the shore, though the rest of the fleet had been dispersed. Soldiers are said to have beckoned him ashore with news of his success, but the wary Henry turned his ship around and returned to Brittany.

Richard's parliament in 1484 attainted ninety-seven individuals for their part in this rebellion. They were predominantly southern and mainly knights, esquires and gentlemen so the revolt might be described as both southern and middle-class in nature. The attachment of Buckingham's name to the rebellion possibly derives from the fact that he was the highest-ranking member of the plot. The 1484 parliament also identified him as a prime mover, perhaps reflecting Richard's sense of betrayal or that with Buckingham dead, it made the revolt appear decisively crushed if it was his plot. In reality, Buckingham joined the scheme very late in the day, apparently talked into it by John Morton, Bishop of Ely, who had been Buckingham's prisoner since his arrest at the Council meeting at which Hastings had been executed.

The rebellion began with the stated aim of freeing the sons of Edward IV and putting Edward V back on the throne. At some point, this goal was altered to placing Henry Tudor on the throne instead. *The Crowland Chronicle* explains that as part of the rebellion, rumours were spread that the Princes were dead so that Tudor could become the figurehead. Those who had been close to Edward IV were courted and as part of the plot, Henry Tudor promised to marry Edward IV's oldest daughter, Elizabeth of York, giving these Yorkist supporters a vested interest in the idea of Tudor as king. It is known that Margaret Beaufort negotiated this arrangement with Elizabeth Woodville, still in sanctuary at Westminster, through a physician, Dr Lewis Caerleon. It is possible that Margaret fed Elizabeth the story of her sons' deaths, even if it wasn't true, to get her to agree to the idea of Henry as king.

Buckingham's Rebellion is something of a misnomer. In reality, this was a revolt by those who had been loyal to Edward IV and Edward V and who opposed Richard, but which was highjacked by an emerging Tudor faction that aimed to replace Richard with Henry Tudor. The rebellion was a serious and dangerous one. Had Kent not risen early and the weather not turned in Richard's favour, it might have succeeded in removing him from the throne after just three months.

Little known fact:

Buckingham had taken part in Edward IV's 1475 campaign to France but had left when it became clear that Edward would pursue peace and agree to the Treaty of Picquigny. It seems feasible that Richard identified with Buckingham and went to him at the emergence of potential problems on Edward IV's death because he thought they shared a view of Edward's abandonment of the campaign.

Chapter 6

The Business of Ruling

Is It True That Richard III Invented Bail?

One of the most contentious arguments about Richard III is the claim made by some that he invented bail and the derisive dismissal of the notion by others. As with so many things in Richard III's story, the truth lies somewhere in the middle.

Richard III certainly did not invent bail. In medieval England, bail was an amount set by the local sheriff for the release of a criminal until trial. The amount was meant to be high enough to ensure that the offender would attend their hearing in order to avoid losing the sum. As early as 1275, the Statute of Westminster limited the power of a sheriff to use bail, codifying which crimes could be subject to bail and which could not.

In 1484, Parliament sought to improve bail and identified the inequity of the system as it stood. The Parliament Rolls record that 'various people are arrested and imprisoned daily on suspicion of felony, sometimes out of malice and sometimes on vague suspicion, and thus kept in prison without bail or mainprise to their great vexation and trouble.' Mainprise was a surety similar to bail, and the complaint was the access to bail was being denied, presumably by corrupt sheriffs. Parliament gave justices of the peace the power to grant bail at the time of arrest as though the prisoner had already been charged and appeared in their court. The problem this measure seems to be tackling was malicious charges that could see people thrown into prison, costing them not only their freedom but the ability to earn money to feed their family, without any evidence against them.

The act went on to deal with a second issue of inequity in the bail system. It enacted that 'no sheriff or escheator, bailiff of a franchise or any other person shall take or seize the goods of any person arrested on suspicion of felony before the person thus arrested and imprisoned has been convicted or attainted of the felony according to the law'. The issue here was clearly that sheriffs were not only denying bail but they were seizing goods from those accused of a crime. There was then no obligation for those goods to be returned if the person was found innocent, and they might be the tools of a trade or food meant to last the winter so that a malicious false accusation could be used to ruin a man. Parliament altered this law so that goods could only be seized after a conviction, adding that the penalty for breaking this law would be 'forfeiting double the value of the goods thus taken to the person harmed in that respect'.

It is possible that this measure was designed to reduce the number of complaints passing across the Chancellor's desk. It has been suggested that Bishop Russell had been unwilling to continue in the role after Edward IV's death and Richard III's accession, so a measure that might reduce his workload might have helped to convince him to stay on. However, it can also be demonstrated that such concerns were in line with Richard's approach to justice during his time as Duke of Gloucester. We already know that he intervened in the feud between the Harrington and Stanley families to defend those he believed to be in the right and hard done to. There are other examples too, including the cases of Katherine Williamson of Howden in 1472 and John Randson in 1480, both cases in which Richard intervened to try and see justice done.

Richard's Parliament would also seek to prevent the corruption rife in juries by implementing requirements that jurors should be of a fixed level of financial worth so that they would not be so easily bribed. That measure might sound odd to our ears, since jury service does not rely on monetary worth, but in a system riddled with corruption, it was meant to resolve a real problem in delivering justice. The act complained that 'various great difficulties and perjuries occur daily in various counties of England due to false verdicts given in inquisitions and inquiries before sheriffs in their tourns by people of no substance or standing, who do not fear God or the world's shame'. The act requiring jurors to own land to a specified value was designed to make them less open to bribery, and it imposed a significant fine of 40s for each unqualified juror appointed by an official.

Richard III certainly did not invent bail. Nor was this the last reform to a problematic system that was abused at a local level, but together, these changes were critical in making justice more equitable and more available to the common man. They were not undone by subsequent monarchs, suggesting that their value was real and together, they hint at a man interested in justice for those traditionally denied it. It is possible that Richard's willingness to provide access to justice in this way added to opposition to him at higher levels of society. It was the gentry and even the nobility who would lose out if their freedom to abuse the system and their social inferiors was curtailed and it is possible that disaffection with Richard and his government stemmed at least in part from dissatisfaction with his desire to effect change that would reduce the authority of certain sections of society.

Little known fact:

Richard III is also credited with the creation of an early form of legal aid for those unable to fund civil court cases. Those who might otherwise be denied justice because they lacked money were able to bring cases before the Court of Requests, and although there is evidence that a similar system existed in ecclesiastical courts, Richard seems to have been determined to make it available to the common man. Henry VII abolished it as soon as he became king, though it reappeared later, housed at the Palace of Westminster in 1519 by Henry VIII.

Why Did English Merchants Like Richard III's Parliament?

As Duke of Gloucester, Richard had shown a keen interest in the north's trade issues and had attempted to rebalance the trading power of the region against that of London merchants. In his Parliament of 1484, he brought these concerns for English merchants to the national stage with measures that his subjects involved in trade must have revelled in.

Parliament firstly considered the dying, wool and cloth trades, complaining that products 'are imperfect and dishonestly made and manufactured, keeping neither reasonable length nor breadth'. The act required that all wool should be previously soaked and should meet strict size guidelines, providing genuine merchants and their customers with a level playing field and protection from sub-standard goods. Next, Parliament confirmed and extended an act of Edward IV's Parliament in 1483 prohibiting the importing of 'bands, girdles, ribbons, laces, spun or woven caul silk or Cologne silk'. Edward had banned these imports for four years, and Richard's Parliament extended the measure for an additional ten years. This effectively gave English tradesmen a monopoly on producing these goods by preventing foreign competition.

The next act went even further in curtailing the ability of foreign merchants and tradesmen operating in competition with their English counterparts. Foreigners were prohibited from working in a list of protected trades identified as 'girdlers, pointmakers, pinners, pursers, glovers, cutlers, bladesmiths, blacksmiths, spurriers, goldbeaters, painters, saddlers, lorimers, founders, cardmakers, capmakers, wiremongers, weavers, horners, bottlemakers and coppersmiths' and goods made by these trades abroad could also not be sold in England. This further cornered the market for English tradesmen in a raft of areas.

Italian merchants were singled out for particular attention. Parliament enacted a bill that required all Italian merchants to sell all of their goods at wholesale prices to English subjects by 1st May 1485. To rub salt into the wound, the same Italian merchants were then to be obliged to spend all of the proceeds of this sale at English ports, on English goods, before leaving the country. A further act sought to tackle what was described as 'the devious means of the Lombards', merchants from northern Italy. The Parliament Rolls detail the accusation that the 'craft of bowyers is seriously reduced and likely to be entirely undone' by the import of substandard bow staves by Lombard merchants. At a time when the English longbow had not been entirely supplanted by the gun, the bow remained a mainstay of English armies. The reduction in quality of imported staves and the impact on the English tradition of making bows was a matter of national security and was, the bill explained 'to the great comfort of its enemies and adversaries'. To correct this perceived problem, all merchants importing wine were required to 'bring ten bow staves of good and suitable material' with every butt of wine imported. The fine for failing to do so was set at 13s 4d per butt without acceptable bowstaves. Malmsey, a strong, sweet, fortified wine very popular in England, could no longer be imported unless the barrel contained 'the old measure' of one butt because it was claimed that foreign merchants were reducing their measures to make their goods go farther for the same price.

When Parliament granted taxation to Richard, it made a clear demarcation between the duties to be paid to the crown by English merchants and the amounts due from those from other nations. On every tun of wine, an English subject was required to pay 3s duty whilst a foreign merchant had to pay 6s. For each 20s worth of other goods, an English merchant was required to pay 1s, and a foreign merchant had to pay 2s. Some items were excluded from any duty, including exports of wool cloth, wool, woolfells, hides and ale or victuals sent to Calais. The import of corn, flour, fresh fish, meat and wine was also exempted from duty. Parliament set the fine for avoidance or evasion of these duties at double the amount of duty owed. The wool trade, so critical to England's medieval economy, was also explicitly tackled. For each sack of wool, an English merchant was to pay a subsidy to the crown of 33s 4d and a foreign merchant 66s 8d. For every 240 woolfells, English merchants would again pay 33s 4d and foreign merchants double, 66s 8d. On every last of hides and English merchant would pay 66s 8d and a foreign merchant 73s 4d.

All of these measures would have been incredibly popular with Richard's subjects involved in any of the trades receiving beneficial treatment against their foreign competitors. All kings received taxation and customs income set by Parliament, but foreign merchants were identified in 1484 for heavy taxation compared to their English counterparts. These measures might reflect a need to court his subjects, but they may also signify the renewal of nationalism, or at least caution, in the face of renewed aggression from France and a willingness to overtly favour and protect English merchants and tradesmen, maintaining jobs and expertise within the country. An increasingly literate and influential merchant and middle class may have been able to bring some pressure to bear to have their grievances heard, but might also have provided a potential foil to the nobility whose power and influence many of Richard's measures sought to reduce. One thing is certain, though. English tradesmen and merchants benefitted from the measures of Richard III's Parliament.

Little known fact:

Medieval weights and measures had some odd names that are not used anymore. A butt of wine was a standardised barrel containing 126 gallons. A woolfell was the skin of a wool-bearing animal with the wool still attached. A last was a standardised shipload. These weights and measures were allegedly being corrupted by foreign merchants to the detriment of English tradesmen, and so they were reinforced by Parliament in 1484.

Chapter 7

Personal Disasters

Who Did Richard III Appoint As His Heir In 1484?

There are two competing schools of thought about who precisely Richard III appointed as his heir after the death of his only legitimate son Edward of Middleham in 1484. Some claim that Richard appointed his young nephew Edward, Earl of Warwick, the son of his older brother George, Duke of Clarence. Others insist that Warwick's age and his father's status as an attainted traitor, which had, after all, barred Warwick from the succession, preclude this and insist that Richard's oldest male nephew, John de la Pole, Earl of Lincoln was in fact appointed as his heir. The truth is very different but perhaps shouldn't be surprising.

Richard had two acknowledged illegitimate children, John of Gloucester (sometimes also called John of Pontefract) and Katherine. The mother of these two children is not known, nor is it certain whether they shared a mother or not, but they appear to have been born before Richard's marriage to Anne. John was knighted by Richard in 1483 and appointed Captain of Calais in 1485, providing him with an important position and a good income. His fate is uncertain after his father's death, but sources tend to suggest he was taken prisoner by Henry VII and did not live long afterwards. Katherine made a prestigious marriage in 1484 to William Herbert, Earl of Pembroke, who received an annual income of £1,000 from the king. Her fate is equally uncertain, though it is generally assumed she was dead by 1487, when Herbert attended the coronation of Elizabeth of York as Henry VII's queen alone. Although acknowledged and well provided for by their father, neither John nor Katherine were realistic options to succeed their father because of their illegitimacy.

Edward, Earl of Warwick was just nine years old when his cousin Edward of Middleham died. His father, George, Duke of Clarence had been executed in February 1478, a week before Edward's third birthday. Titulus Regius, which outlined and confirmed Richard III's title to the crown, had stated that George's attainder meant that Edward too was disqualified from the throne. Unless and until the attainder against George was reversed by Parliament he was still prevented from inheriting. Richard would have faced a serious problem in undoing the attainder affected Warwick in that it would hand Warwick a superior claim to Richard's own as a more senior male-line descendant of the House of York.

Warwick had been placed within the household of the Council of the North, based in Richard's former heartlands and appears to have been not only well treated but also prepared for a role in politics, even though he was still too young to take an active part. Records from the city of York show that when officials wrote to the Council, letters were addressed to the Earl of Warwick above all other names. Although Warwick's rehabilitation might pose its own problems, it seems that Richard was investing in his nephew and that he may well have planned to integrate him into political life in the future, meaning that he could have represented a serious option as Richard's heir.

John de la Pole, Earl of Lincoln was the oldest son of Richard's sister, Elizabeth, Duchess of Suffolk. Elizabeth was married to John de la Pole, 2nd Duke of Suffolk. Lincoln's date of birth is unclear, but he would have been in his very early twenties by the time Edward of Middleham passed away. Lincoln was the oldest male heir of the House of York, though his descent was through the female line of his mother, making it arguably weaker. However, Elizabeth was older than George, and the entire claim of the House of York through the Mortimer line relied on the ability to pass a claim on through a female line. While descent in the male line was still preferable, Edward III had claimed the throne of France through his mother Isabella and Richard, Duke of York relied on his Mortimer descent through a granddaughter of Edward III to claim a better right to the crown than Henry VI.

The death of Edward of Middleham in the Spring of 1484 created a crisis for Richard almost immediately after Parliament had confirmed him as king, dealt with the aftermath of the October Rebellion and Elizabeth Woodville had released her daughters from sanctuary to join the king's court. Just as matters seemed to be settling down, dynastic crisis reared its head. Richard would have been all too aware of the need to resolve this issue as quickly as possible, not least because of the events that had led to him becoming king. However, it was not quite that simple.

It is a matter of record that Richard was negotiating for a new marriage alliance with either Spain or Portugal, with the Portuguese match seeming the most likely. The primary purpose of this union, alongside other considerations, would have been to secure an heir for Richard as quickly as possible to avert this crisis that threatened to loom over Richard's kingship for almost twenty years, until a son could be born and come of age. If this was where Richard's hope lay, he would not have wished to muddy the waters or complicate the matter by naming another member of his family as his heir. To do so would be to create a time bomb, since if Richard succeeded in having another son, he would have to disinherit a relative who, even if they had understood the position to be temporary, might feel aggrieved by a sudden reduction in their standing. After all, that was precisely what had caused George, Duke of Clarence to leave Warwick's side during their rebellion when Warwick's alliance with Margaret of Anjou made his path to the throne a much more distant possibility. It may even have lain at the heart of Clarence's original revolt against Edward IV, having been considered his heir until his son, Edward V, was born in 1470. Richard would have known, or at least hoped, that he would be giving a gift he would have to take back, and that would be to store up problems for the future and perhaps for the son he hoped to father.

There is debate over the identity of Richard III's heir after the death of his only legitimate son because there is no documentary evidence available to prove what decision was made, and more importantly, whether any decision or declaration was made at all. In strict legal terms, it is most likely that Lincoln would have been considered Richard's heir presumptive because of Clarence's attainder still barring his son Warwick. Lincoln was also a grown man and was becoming an experienced governor in the north just as Richard himself had done. Many would not hope for a minor to take the throne again and Warwick had many years before he might be considered of age. Lincoln had the advantage of age, experience and seniority. Richard did not need to make any declaration as to the identity of his heir. To do so would not only acknowledge his own dynastic weakness but it would store up problems for the future. There was a legal principle in place that meant people would have understood Lincoln to be Richard's theoretical heir, if needed, without the king needing to embarrass himself, tie his hands or create a problem for himself. Henry VI had been enraged when an MP requested that Richard, Duke of York be recognised as his heir. Elizabeth I would famously refuse to address the question as well. Richard III appointed neither Warwick nor Lincoln as his heir formally because he had no need to say anything on the matter.

Little known fact

There were two kinds of heir during the medieval period. An heir apparent was the oldest surviving legitimate son whose legal claim to his father's titles and estates could not be overturned by another family member. The heir presumptive was a more distant family member such as a younger brother or nephew who stood to inherit until the arrival of an heir apparent. The position of an heir presumptive could, therefore, be lost to an heir apparent.

Did Richard III Poison His Wife?

Richard III's personal life was to be touched by tragedy during his time as king. His only legitimate child, Edward of Middleham, Prince of Wales died in April 1484, and although Richard had two acknowledged illegitimate children, John and Katherine, his dynastic future rested on a legitimate son. The loss of Edward at the age of ten was a severe blow not only personally to the king and queen, who were reported by the Crowland Chronicle as being devastated, but also to Richard's stability as king with an heir to succeed him. It must have been early in 1485 that Richard's wife of more than ten years, Anne Neville, also fell ill and she would die on 16 March 1485. Shakespeare famously has his Richard kill his wife by poison, but did the king really murder the queen?

Anne Neville was born on 11 June 1456, the younger daughter of Richard Neville, the Earl of Warwick, known as the Kingmaker. Warwick

Middleham Castle, North Yorkshire, where Richard stayed during his time in the Earl of Warwick's household and where he was based during his own time in the north after 1471. (Author's collection)

had been Richard's guardian as a boy, and we know that Richard and Anne met at least once during that period when they are recorded sitting at the same table during the feast to celebrate the enthronement of Warwick's brother George Neville as Archbishop of York in 1465. It seems possible that they saw each other on other occasions, though it is perhaps fanciful to date any romantic attachment to this period. It is not impossible, though, particularly if Richard had been fond of Anne and felt the urge to protect her after her father's death in 1471.

Warwick's elder daughter Isabel had been married to Richard's brother George, Duke of Clarence against the instructions of Edward IV as part of their plot to remove him from the throne. When Warwick made an alliance with Margaret of Anjou, Henry VI's queen, in 1470, Anne was married to Henry's son Edward of Westminster, Prince of Wales as part of the deal. When Edward was killed at the Battle of Tewkesbury, Anne was widowed and probably in the spring of 1472, she married Richard, who was taking control of much of her father's northern patrimony. There is nothing to suggest that their marriage was not a happy one, though they had only one child, Edward of Middleham, born in 1473.

Shakespeare's Richard III instructs Catesby 'Rumour it abroad that Anne, my wife, is sick and like to die' as part of his scheme to poison her. In this, Shakespeare draws on contemporary rumours that Richard planned to kill his wife so that he could marry his own niece, Elizabeth of York. Anne appears as one of the ghosts who haunt Richard's dreams the night before the Battle of Bosworth, but it is most likely that Anne died of tuberculosis, then called consumption, the disease which it was believed killed her sister Isabel in 1476. Reports circulated that Richard was shunning their marital bed out of cruelty to his wife, a story used to add fuel to the rumours that he planned to kill her. If Anne did develop tuberculosis, it seems likely that all of the medical advice would have been for Richard to keep his distance from the highly contagious and fatal disease his wife had contracted.

There are later reports of Richard weeping at Anne's funeral, but there is no contemporary evidence that he attended the service, not an unusual fact in the medieval period, never mind that he wept. This story seems to have been added as a later flourish to portray them as a happy couple and Richard as a devoted husband who would never have murdered his wife. Both of these things may be true, but there is no real evidence to reinforce the view. On 30 March 1485, two weeks after Anne's death, Richard made a speech reported in the *Acts of Court of the Mercers' Company*. He denied that he planned to marry his niece and insisted he was 'nor willing nor glad of the death of his queen but as sorry and in the heart as heavy as man might be'. This suggests both that he did love his wife, or at least wanted it known that he did, and that the rumour of some foul play in her death was current shortly after she passed away.

The accusation may have followed on from the death of the couple's only son. After more than ten years of marriage with only one child, it may have seemed unlikely that the couple would have more children, endangering Richard's dynasty. Anne was just twenty-eight years old, but concern over the couple's ability to have more children would make their position on the throne precarious. Given the nature of the plot in late 1483 and the invasion that would come during 1485, it is possible that rumours of Richard trying to kill his wife, like those about the murders of the Princes in the Tower, were spread as part of the continuing plot to promote Henry Tudor and remove Richard from the throne. Although it remains impossible to be sure, the likelihood is that the story of Richard murdering his wife is a fiction that became readily accepted in Shakespeare's retelling and as part of the dark reputation that was to swallow Richard.

Little known fact:

On the day that Anne Neville died, 16th March 1485, there was a solar eclipse. In a superstitious age, such a thing might well have been taken as a bad omen for the remainder of Richard's kingship. It was reported in chronicles that at the time Richard, Duke of York's claim to the throne was declared better than Henry VI's in Parliament in 1460, a crown mysteriously fell from the ceiling of the House of Commons where it had decorated a branch. At the same time, another crown fell from the top of Dover Castle for no apparent reason. Both of these were taken as ill omens for Henry VI's kingship.

Did Richard III Plan To Marry His Niece?

One of the most insidious and persistent stories about Richard III is that he planned to marry his niece, Elizabeth of York, immediately after the death of his wife, Anne Neville. The motive for wishing to make this match is cited as the support Elizabeth drew as her father's heir, particularly if her brothers were at least believed to be dead. This rumour is based on very little yet is readily accepted by many historians, so how likely is it that Richard might have planned to marry his niece in 1485?

Shakespeare makes this notion a fact in his play. When Richard orders Catesby to spread the rumour of Anne's illness, he also explains that he plans to marry George, Duke of Clarence's daughter, Margaret, to 'some mean-born gentleman', that George's son Edward, Earl of Warwick 'is foolish, and I fear him not'. When Catesby has gone, Richard adds 'I must be married to my brother's daughter, or else my kingdom stands on brittle glass'. Richard did not marry his niece Margaret to 'some mean-born gentleman'. Henry VII married her to one of his distant cousins Sir Richard Pole in 1487, and the story of Warwick being 'foolish' seems to originate from a later Tudor source. *Hall's Chronicle*, published in 1548, claimed that after so many years as a prisoner 'he coulde not descerne a Goose from a Capon'. There is no contemporary evidence that Warwick was in any way 'foolish' and Richard seemed to have been preparing him for an active role in politics within the Council of the North.

Combined with the murder of Anne, this brief passage appears to contain three falsehoods in the four charges, so should the notion that Richard sought security by marrying his niece be as easily dismissed as a fourth fiction? The evidence offered for the existence of such a plan is twofold. Firstly, there were contemporary rumours. In the same speech, reported in the *Acts of Court of the Mercers' Company*, in which Richard spoke of his sorrow at Anne's death, the king made an explicit denial that he intended to marry his niece. The account records that Richard 'showed his grief and displeasure aforesaid and said it never came into his thought or mind to marry in such manner wise'. This suggests that there was a belief Richard might make such a marriage after Anne's death. It is believed that two of his closest advisors, Sir Richard Ratcliffe and Sir William Catesby counselled him to publicly deny the damaging allegation, though it is to be wondered whether the denial did more harm than the rumour.

The second piece of evidence provided for the story is a record of a letter, said to be in Elizabeth of York's hand, which might be interpreted as referring to her intention to marry her uncle Richard. The note does not survive but was reported by Sir George Buck, and its contents only remain in a partial, fire damaged copy within Buck's manuscript. The letter was reportedly sent by Elizabeth to John Howard, Duke of Norfolk, one of Richard's key supporters, in February 1485, before Anne's death, and refers to Norfolk acting as a 'mediator for her to the K…[text missing]', describing him as 'her onely joy and maker'. The fragment contains a final reference 'that she feared the Queene would neu…' which is too damaged to be read, but which has been interpreted as meaning she feared the queen would never die. The reported existence of this letter from Elizabeth does not prove that Richard planned to marry her since the words do not come from him. If Elizabeth wrote such a letter to one of Richard's key supporters, it is possible that it was designed to stir up the very trouble that followed it as part of a whispering campaign against

Richard by the Tudor faction possibly with Elizabeth's involvement, since success would make her queen.

It is a documented truth that following Anne's death, Richard stepped up negotiations to marry either a Portuguese or Spanish princess, with the favoured candidate appearing to be Joanna of Portugal, who was the same age as Richard. The negotiations included plans to marry Elizabeth of York to Joanna's cousin Manuel, who would later become King Manuel I of Portugal. Such an arrangement would have been in line with Richard's promise to find suitable marriages for his nieces and may have been a better match than expected for illegitimate daughters. It would also serve to negate the threat of Henry Tudor's promise to marry her. It is possible that these arrangements were misinterpreted, deliberately or otherwise, as a plan for Richard to marry his niece himself.

Marriage to a close family member was by no means usual, even within the higher nobility of the medieval period. Richard and Anne had been cousins, and that degree of relationship was accepted, and often unavoidable, but an uncle marrying his niece would have been considered beyond the pale and Richard would have been well aware of that. Rather than improving his position, the mere rumour of the idea served to weaken him and has haunted his reputation ever since. There is no firm evidence that Richard ever intended to make the match and the negotiations with Spain and Portugal go a long way to proving that he did not intend it. Richard had an interest in seeing Elizabeth married off so that she could not be used by Henry Tudor to threaten him, but he had apparently found a way to achieve this without marrying her himself.

Little known fact:

The earliest surviving portrait of Richard III is a later copy, made after his death, but is believed to be a reproduction of a portrait produced to be sent to Spain and Portugal as part of the negotiations to remarry. The royal families of Spain and Portugal had Lancastrian blood which would have served to unite the houses of York and Lancaster just as Henry VII planned to. John of Gaunt was Joanna of Portugal's great-great-grandfather on both her father and mother's side.

Why Was Richard III Unpopular?

It is an odd thing that a man who was King of England for just over two years should attract more attention than most other monarchs spanning the centuries. Opinion is divided by Richard III today between those who believe he is guilty of at least most, if not all, of the charges laid at his feet by history and those who consider him a wronged man, a victim of Tudor propaganda who would have been a great king had he been given time. The evidence suggests that this very argument was raging during his reign, when he inspired devotion and hatred in equal measure.

Richard III seems to have inspired a deep loyalty in those he might have considered closest to him. Many, including John Howard, Duke of Norfolk, Sir Richard Ratcliffe and Sir Robert Brackenbury would die alongside him at the Battle of Bosworth, yet the presence of an invading army swollen by disaffected former supporters of his brother Edward IV shows that he had been unable to inspire such devotion on a broader scale. There were several barriers placed in Richard's path to wider acceptance as king that he was unable to get over.

Although Richard should be considered a national figure, as a royal duke, brother to a king, Lord High Constable, Lord High Admiral and a respected military man, he was also, at least to those in London, a northerner and an unknown quantity. At his arrival in London in 1483, there was some concern and confusion because Richard was not well known in the city as many of the other key figures such as Lord Hastings, Elizabeth Woodville and her son Thomas Grey, Marquis of Dorset. This meant that no one was quite sure what to expect from Richard, particularly at a time when the north-south divide in England was deeply entrenched and reinforced with prejudices about northern barbarity and southern scheming. After the October Rebellion, Richard drew men from the north, who he trusted, to replace those who had rebelled and this northern takeover only increased the nervous suspicion of the northern king.

The nature of Richard's arrival on the throne would also necessarily cause him problems. Edward IV had overseen a period of stability and economic growth that was unprecedented in living memory. His son had been prepared from birth to succeed his father, and for twelve years, everyone had expected Edward V to follow his father. The same people probably expected another twenty years of Edward IV's rule first, though. The king's unexpected early death, his son's status as a minor, the fresh aggression from France and Scotland and the power play in London between Lord Hastings, the Woodville family and Richard was a shock to the political system. In sweeping away the security and expectations of the previous years, Richard could not avoid sowing uncertainty of the kind that made people nervous. On top of that, he openly and vehemently criticised his brother's style of government and those who delivered it, leaving him little alternative but to try and sweep away the political establishment he so roundly condemned. This naturally meant driving those closest to Edward IV into political opposition, and Richard failed to foresee their willingness to fight against him after they had lost their positions and wealth.

Richard's intentions might also have caused many to oppose him as king. In Parliament, he had taken steps to improve the inequity inherent in the system of bastard feudalism and livery and maintenance. As Duke of Gloucester, he had frequently acted against the vested interests of those higher on the social ladder in favour of those suffering lower down. The actions against fishgarths, efforts to improve northern trade and measures taken against his retainers in favour of justice might seem indulgent in his own northern power base, but on a national level, they posed a real threat to those with anything to lose. Preventing corruption in courts and on juries whilst providing access to an early form of legal aid in civil courts to assist those who could not afford to fund their cause threatened those who benefitted from that corruption and from the inequity that they relied on. Richard's reforms caused fear that cost him support, in part because he was not smart or subtle enough in trying to deliver them.

There is evidence that Richard tried to be inclusive and unifying in his approach despite his lambasting of his brother's government. He failed to attaint Lady Margaret Beaufort for her part in the October Rebellion and rewarded her husband with custody of her vast wealth. Elizabeth Woodville and her daughters were brought out of sanctuary with a promise to care for them. For a man often considered ruthless and dangerous, it was perhaps a lack of these qualities that allowed his real enemies to continue to prosper and work against him to bring about his eventual downfall.

Thomas Langton, Bishop of St David's, famously wrote to the Prior of Christ Church in September 1483, during Richard's royal progress, that

'He contents the people wherever he goes better than ever did any prince; for many a poor man that has suffered wrongs many days has been relieved and helped by him and his commands in his progress'. And in many great cities and towns were sums of money given to him which he has refused. On my faith I never liked the qualities of a prince as well as his; God has sent him to us for the welfare of us all'. There is a strong sense that Richard could inspire personal loyalty in some, but that he could not gain the acceptance of those whose support he really needed to maintain

Lady Margaret Beaufort, wife of Thomas, Lord Stanley and mother of Henry Tudor, later King Henry VII. Margaret was involved in rebellion against Richard in October 1483 and saw her son win the throne in 1485. Portrait by a Follower of Maynard Waynwyk. (Public domain image via Wikimedia Commons)

his position on the throne and that perhaps he was perceived as a threat to the power those men held.

Little known fact:

Thomas Langton remained in favour despite his high praise of King Richard III. Before Richard's death, Thomas became Bishop of Salisbury, and Henry VII later transferred him to Winchester. On 22 January 1501, Thomas was elected Archbishop of Canterbury, but he died of the plague five days later before he was officially confirmed in the office. His effusive praise of Richard III doesn't seem to have hampered his career after Richard's death.

Chapter 8

The Battle of Bosworth Field

Who Betrayed Richard III At The Battle Of Bosworth?

The odds at the Battle of Bosworth on 22 August 1485 seemed to be heavily in Richard III's favour. Betrayal and treason are charges frequently blamed for Richard's loss and death at Bosworth, but can we see clearly who actually betrayed the king?

Henry Tudor had landed at Mill Bay in south-west Wales on 7th August and marched north along the Welsh coast before turning east and appearing to head for London. He had arrived with a small force of French and Scottish mercenaries, bolstered by those who had left England during Richard's reign. One of the first betrayals of Richard came from his representative in south Wales, Sir Rhys ap Thomas, who had the responsibility for opposing any invasion there. There is a story that Sir Rhys had sworn to Richard that any attack would have to take place over his body and that when Henry Tudor landed, Sir Rhys stood beneath a bridge whilst Henry passed over, thus fulfilling his vow. The story appears in a much later source, and it is unclear whether it is true or not, but Sir Rhys, who went on to become a powerful and trusted ally to Henry VII, certainly betrayed Richard III weeks before Bosworth.

Support had been slower to come in Wales than Henry might have hoped, but by the time he reached Bosworth, he probably had around 5,000 men with him. Estimates of Richard's force give him around 8-12,000 men, with about 4,000 of those under the control of Henry Percy, Earl of Northumberland, acting as the rearguard in case reinforcements were needed. Thomas Stanley and his brother Sir William brought between 4,000 and 6,000 men and positioned themselves a short distance from both armies, allowing them to give the impression that they might support either side.

Richard had the advantage in terms of artillery and after cannon fire and an archery exchange, the two vanguards led by John Howard, Duke of Norfolk for Richard and John de Vere, Earl of Oxford for Henry Tudor engaged. Oxford gained the upper hand, and Norfolk was killed, the falling of his standard sowing fear and panic amongst his men and making it hard to keep them disciplined, despite the presence of Norfolk's son Thomas Howard, Earl of Surrey. Records for the battle are poor and provide little detail, but it is believed that Richard ordered the rearguard to move up and reinforce Norfolk's vanguard, but Henry Percy, Earl of Northumberland failed to advance.

It has been suggested either that Northumberland was prevented from moving by marshy ground in front of him, which would make the initial deployment of the rearguard a disastrous tactical failure, or that he did not engage because he had decided to betray Richard. The Percy family had been staunch Lancastrians throughout the Wars of the Roses, but the 4th Earl who was present at Bosworth had regained favour under Edward IV and had been granted the earldom from John Neville. It is possible that latent Lancastrian sympathies drove him to consider favouring Henry. With Richard's accession in 1483 and his removal from the north, where he had been the dominant political force for over a decade, Northumberland may also have expected an increase in his own authority. The continued use of the Council of the North under the leadership of John de la Pole, Earl of Lincoln and Clarence's young son Edward, Earl of Warwick surely disabused him of such a notion. Resentment at the failure to regain what he deemed his rightful position in the north might also have caused Northumberland to wonder whether his future might not be brighter under Henry Tudor.

If Northumberland did betray Richard at Bosworth and fail to move when ordered, Henry Tudor appears to have been unaware of his defection. Tudor had been in contact with several factions since his landing and Northumberland, like many others, may have decided to try and back Henry if the opportunity arose, but also to keep his plans to himself so that if Richard was victorious, he could reap the rewards of loyalty. Following Bosworth, Northumberland was arrested and spent several months imprisoned in the Tower of London before Henry VII finally released him and allowed him to keep his former lands, titles and

Richard III charges into battle at the annual re-enactment of the Battle of Bosworth at the Bosworth Battlefield Heritage Centre. (Author's collection)

Richard III is struck down during the fighting at the Battle of Bosworth re-enactment weekend. (Author's collection)

offices. His participation in a diplomatic mission suggests that he was entirely trusted by the new king after a short period. Northumberland met his end on 28 April 1487 when a tax rebellion in Yorkshire he sought to quell led to his lynching by the rebels. It has been suggested ever since that the men of Yorkshire had never forgiven the earl for his betrayal of their beloved king less than two years earlier, so there seems to have been contemporary feeling that Northumberland had turned his coat at Bosworth and failed to support Richard in a deliberate act of treachery.

More certain is the betrayal of Thomas, Lord Stanley. Thomas is believed to have met with his stepson Henry Tudor before Bosworth and pledged his allegiance. Richard was, perhaps unsurprisingly, suspicious of Thomas and took his son, Lord Strange, as a hostage for his father's good behaviour. Thomas Stanley claimed to be too ill to come to the king himself – he had perhaps contracted the infamous sweating sickness that Henry's army brought across with it when he met his stepson before the day of Bosworth. Instead, he gave assurances of his loyalty, though asserted that keeping Lord Strange hostage would do Richard no good because he had other sons anyway. It was Thomas's brother Sir William Stanley, most likely on the orders of his older brother, who drove his men into Richard's and decisively ended the battle. Thomas would be made Earl of Derby as a reward for his part, a title his descendants still hold today. Whether this willingness to betray Richard stemmed from a distaste for his rule, a belief he had killed his nephews or a decision that he would prosper far more with his stepson on the throne than a man he had quarrelled with a decade and a half earlier over Hornby Castle is impossible to tell. Thomas Stanley's betrayal was key to Richard's loss at Bosworth, though.

Little known fact:

Many men who had served Richard for a long time remained utterly loyal at Bosworth and died at his side, including Sir Richard Ratcliffe and Sir Robert Brackenbury. Sir Percival Thirlwall, Richard's standard bearer, possibly best sums up the intense personal loyalty Richard was able to inspire, but which he could never translate to a national stage. Sir Percival had both his legs cut from beneath him in the fierce melee that followed Richard's cavalry charge, but he kept the king's standard vertical and flying until his own death to show that Richard was not yet, quite, defeated.

Did Richard III Call For A Horse To Flee Bosworth?

'A horse! A horse! My kingdom for a horse!' is perhaps one of the most famous lines of Shakespeare's Richard III, interpreted by many to signify Richard's personal cowardice as the Battle of Bosworth Field turned against him. If that were what Shakespeare was trying to portray, it would be at odds with every other contemporary or later source, but cowardice is not something even Shakespeare accuses Richard of.

Sources for the way in which the Battle of Bosworth was actually fought on 22 August 1485 are scant and offer general overviews, providing little more detail than that Henry won and Richard was killed. John de Vere, Earl of Oxford, who led Henry Tudor's army, would later claim that he had used a tactic of rotating the two vanguards when they met to put the sun in the eyes of Richard's force, blinding them and increasing Oxford's advantage. It was a manoeuvre that had been in existence in Roman times and which fifteenth-century writers still advocated, but it appears in Vergil's account, written some twenty years after the battle. It is possible Oxford himself was a source for the story and that he could have cemented his own military legend by claiming he had used such ancient wisdom. It is also a plausible explanation for the swift victory of Oxford's vanguard over that led by John Howard, Duke of Norfolk, who was killed in the melee.

It is reported that Richard spotted Henry Tudor's banner moving across the rear of the battlefield towards the position taken up by the Stanley forces of his stepfather. Guessing that Henry meant to try and convince Thomas Stanley to join the fray on his side, Richard led a charge of his household cavalry, which might have been as many as 200 men thundering across the ground in shining plate armour with their lances aimed at their enemies. The largely French contingent around Henry resisted the onslaught, possibly using a formation known as the hedgehog in which their polearms offered a bristling barrier against the cavalry. Eventually, with the arrival of Sir William Stanley's men, Richard's group was overwhelmed and he himself was killed.

Despite the traditional cowardly reputation Richard has been bequeathed by Shakespeare, even the most hostile contemporary and near-contemporary sources praise his bravery at Bosworth. *The Crowland Chronicle*, the continuation for this period written in 1486 by an author who was no fan of Richard's, recorded that 'in the thick of the fight, and not in the act of flight, King Richard fell in the field, struck by many mortal wounds, as a bold and most valiant prince'. John Rous, the historian of the Earls of Warwick who had been effusive in his praise for Richard during the king's lifetime, but who had quickly collected and rewritten his manuscripts on Henry VII accession, was similarly forced to concede that Richard had died bravely. He recorded in his hostile version that 'if I may say the truth to his credit, though small in body and feeble of limb, he bore himself like a gallant knight and acted with distinction as his own champion until his last breath, shouting oftentimes that he was betrayed and crying "Treason! Treason! Treason!"'.

Polydore Vergil, who wrote in the early sixteenth century and painted Richard as an evil villain, could not deny the former king a brave death. His words are perhaps the most complimentary, conveying in a few simple words the fall of a man he had written nothing else good about. Vergil recorded that 'King Richard, alone, was killed fighting manfully in the thickest press of his enemies'. Foreign writers who were not based in England appear to have heard similar good reports of Richard's final moments. Jean Molinet noted that 'The king bore himself valiantly according to his destiny'. The account given by Diego de Valera, a Spanish ambassador, in early 1486 perhaps provides the basis for the version Shakespeare wrote. de Valera reported that when the battle began to go badly, a squire named Salazar counselled Richard to flee the battle. The king reportedly responded to the advice by saying 'Salazar, God forbid I yield one step. This day I will die as king or win'. The king, wearing a royal crown atop his helmet, 'began to fight with much vigour, putting heart into those that remained loyal, so that by his sole effort he upheld the battle for a long time.'

The Shakespeare line 'A horse! A horse! My kingdom for a horse!' only portrays Richard as a coward if it is taken entirely out of context. During the battle portrayed in the play, Richard finds William Catesby and delivers the infamous line. Catesby, mistaking the king's meaning, replies 'Withdraw, my lord; I'll help you to a horse.' Richard, frustrated, replies 'Slave, I have set my life upon a cast, And I will stand the hazard of the die', demonstrating that he has no intention of fleeing but means to see out the battle. He continues 'I think there be six Richmonds in the field; Five have I slain to-day instead of him. A horse! a horse! my kingdom for a horse!' Richard explains that he has already killed five men he believed to be Henry Tudor (Earl of Richmond) and he demands a horse in order to return to the fighting to find his enemy. The line so often misinterpreted as a jibe at Richard for cowardice is, in fact, in line with all other reports, even the most hostile, which state that whatever his failings, Richard died bravely on the battlefield.

Edward Hall, a later Tudor antiquary, perhaps summed up the inability to condemn Richard on a charge of cowardice and perhaps many of the other crimes he is accused of. He wrote simply that 'to God which knew his interior cogitations at the hour of his death, I remit the punishment of his offences committed in his life.' Any attempt by Richard to flee the Battle of Bosworth is a fiction both odd and cruel because it relies on a misinterpretation of Shakespeare and is directly contradictory to even the most hostile reporter's version of the brave death in the thick of the fighting of the last English king to die in battle.

Little known fact:

Amongst Henry Tudor's army was a knight named Sir John Cheney. Sir John had been a loyal supporter of Edward IV, one of those unable to reconcile himself to the rule of Richard III who had joined Henry Tudor. Sir John stood 6'8" tall, a giant of a man, yet Richard bested him in single combat at the Battle of Bosworth, leaving Sir John unhorsed and injured. An impressive feat for a man more than a foot shorter, hampered by scoliosis and who John Rous described as 'small in body and feeble of limb'.

What Happened To Richard's Body After Bosworth?

The discovery of Richard III's remains in a Leicester car park in 2012 has provided a wealth of detailed information about what happened to Richard III's body at the Battle of Bosworth and in the aftermath of

Henry Tudor's victory. Several stories had existed about Richard's final resting place and the fate of his remains, which can now be settled by some cold, hard facts.

Richard's skeleton showed a number of serious wounds, some inflicted before death, one or two believed to have been the cause of death and some delivered after death as a means of degrading his body. A wound to the base of the right-hand side of Richard's skull may have been fatal. It was probably delivered by a sword, and a mark opposite on the inside of the skull shows that it penetrated deeply. The blow that is believed to have killed Richard caused a chunk of his skull at the rear to be sliced cleanly off. This wound is consistent with a halberd or similar large, flat, sharp weapon delivering a powerful blow.

The skull shows a further wound from a sharp, pointed weapon to the top of the head that cracked the skull and a circle of bone sliced away to the back left of the skull which is suggestive of a glancing blow from a slicing weapon such as a sword. The lower jaw shows a cut mark on the right-hand side of the chin, and an entry wound on the right cheek has a corresponding exit wound on the left side that suggests a dagger was pushed right through the cheekbone from right to left. These wounds suggest that by the final phase of the battle, Richard had removed or lost his helmet, allowing such serious damage to his skull. Although it is possible some of these blows were delivered after death, it would have been important that Richard's face remained recognisable so that his body could be displayed and his death confirmed.

Two injuries to the body are believed to have been inflicted after Richard's death as a form of punishment or humiliation of his corpse. A cut to the right rib must have been delivered after Richard's armour had been removed and a dagger or sword was driven into the king's right buttock, leaving a mark on the inside of his pelvic bone. Again, this type of injury would be hard to deliver to a man in a full suit of armour. It is consistent with reports that Richard's body was stripped naked and slung over the back of a horse to be taken back to Leicester, at some point during which a dagger could have been thrust into him.

After Henry Tudor's victory, he and his army moved to Leicester, taking the body of Richard III with them. The corpse was put on public display for several days, a typical measure to allow news of the old king's death to be confirmed and spread, preventing rumours that he was still alive from circulating later. It is believed that the brothers of the Franciscan Order of Friars Minor, known as the Greyfriars, approached the new king as he prepared to leave Leicester for London to ask for permission to bury the old king's body. They were allowed to do so but apparently hurried the task, perhaps under pressure from Henry VII. The grave Richard was buried in near the choir of Greyfriars, Leicester was shallow and too short for his body.

For centuries, the location of Richard's remains was uncertain. *The Frowyk Chronicle* reported that he had been buried 'at the Newark', Jean Molinet gave the location as 'a village church' and Sir William Burton said he was thrown 'in a dyke like a dogge'. John Rous appears to have provided the correct location; 'in the choir of the Friars Minor in Leicester'. John Speed added to the problems in the seventeenth century by describing a local legend that Richard's remains had been dug up and thrown into the River Soar during the Reformation, a local myth that had traction for centuries. In 2008, the location was confirmed by Dr John Ashdown-Hill's discovery in the National Archives of a record of Henry VII commissioning a tomb to be built over Richard's grave in 1494 'in the Church of Friers in the town of leycestr where the bones of King Richard IIIde reste'.

The Looking for Richard Project was born from a desire to try and locate this grave and establish where Richard had been buried and whether he was still there. The Project uncovered the most likely position of the Greyfriars Church, which had long been demolished, and engaged the University of Leicester to investigate the archaeology. Not only was the Greyfriars Church found, but the first trench sunk contained the grave of King Richard III. A great deal of controversy followed around where Richard's remains should be reinterred, with York, in particular, making impassioned bids to provide a home for the king.

Eventually, the remains were reinterred at Leicester Cathedral over five days of ceremony beginning on 22 March 2015 with the bones being placed into a lead-lined ossuary and a wooden coffin. The remains travelled from the University of Leicester to the site of the Bosworth Battlefield Heritage Centre before retracing the original journey the body had made to Leicester. From 23-25 March, the coffin was in Leicester

The tomb of King Richard III at Leicester Cathedral, where his mortal remains were reinterred in 2015. (Author's collection)

Cathedral and could be viewed by the public. On 26 March, a reburial service took place in Leicester Cathedral before the tomb was unveiled to the public on 27 March.

The remains of Richard III have shed new light both on the scoliosis he lived with and the injuries that killed him at Bosworth. The tense disputes that surrounded his discovery and reburial clearly demonstrate that even after more than 500 years, Richard III can still inspire passion, hatred and controversy in equal measure.

Little known fact:

Henry VII commissioned a marble tomb to cover Richard III's grave in 1494. A later version of a planned inscription was discovered, but the language and dates are not correct so it may not be genuine. When it came time to rebury Richard, the Richard III Society commissioned a tomb design that was not adopted and instead a plain stone tomb with an incised cross was put in place. The wooden coffin in which the remains rest was built by Michael Ibsen, a collateral descendant of Richard III whose DNA helped to identify the king's remains.

Glossary:

An ossuary is a container, box or even a room specifically designed for the permanent interment of skeletal human remains.

Chapter 9

Richard's Legacy

Did York Defy The Tudors In Richard's Memory?

The attachment felt by the north to King Richard III as a man who had demonstrated good lordship in the region lingers even today. The benefits enjoyed by York and the north of England were clear to see whilst Richard was Duke of Gloucester and his desire to show the area favour may have been behind a good deal of the suspicion of him harboured by those in the south. York was initially willing to resist the loss of the last Yorkist king, but how long could it last as the new regime established itself?

Universal popularity is never something a political figure can claim to enjoy, and the higher the public profile, the more diverse opinion can become. On 24 June 1482, the mayor of York investigated reports of a citizen who was alleged to have claimed that Richard did nothing for their city, though the man denied having said anything at all against the duke. In February 1483, the *York House Book* records another case in which ale-house gossip appears to have turned to Richard's influence in the upcoming mayoral election. A case claimed that Richard wanted Thomas Wrangwish, who had been mayor in 1476, elected whilst another man claimed that if Richard wanted Wrangwish, the people of York would make sure another was selected. For all these little snippets are interesting, they are hardly damning evidence of neglect or corruption. They were gossip that was denied by those accused.

In April 1485, as the summer campaigning season approached and the threat of an invasion by Henry Tudor loomed, Richard wrote letters to be sent throughout the realm complaining about the slanders against him. The *York House Book* records the copy sent to the city, in which the king rails against 'diverse sedicious and evil disposed personnes both in our citie of London and elleswher within this our realme' who were spreading 'false and abhominable langage and lyes' both in speeches and by putting up notices. Richard ordered city officials 'from hensfurth as oft as they find any persone speking of us… othrewise than is according to honour, trouth and the peas and ristfulness of this our realme… they take and arrest the same person… [or] answere unto us at your extreme perill.' This letter was probably sent to all corners of the realm, but the fact that Richard was even beginning to fear sedition in York would have been very worrying.

Perhaps the most famous act of defiance made by the City of York in favour of King Richard III came when news of his defeat and death reached the officials the day after the Battle of Bosworth. The *York House Book* contains an entry from 23 August 1485 which reports solemnly 'King Richard late mercifully reigning upon us was thrugh grete treason of the duc of Northefolk and many othre that turned ayenst hyme, with many othre lordes and nobilles of this north parties, was pitiously slane and murdred to the grete hevynesse of this citie'. The report that the Duke of Norfolk was amongst those who had betrayed Richard is incorrect and demonstrates that in the immediate aftermath of the battle, rumour and false intelligences might have affected the quality of information arriving in the north. Nevertheless, the city officials took a significant risk in describing the defeat of King Richard as treason and betrayal.

Interestingly, the *York House Book* also reveals that on the day after this entry, 24 August 1485, Henry VII's representative was too frightened to enter the city and bring news of the new king's accession. The entry notes that 'Forsomuch as the forsaid Sir Roger Cotam durst not for fere of deth come thrugh the citie to speake with the maire and his brethre, it was thought that they shuld goo unto him', showing that Henry's agent was so terrified he would not enter the city. In what may well have been a further act of defiance, the mayor and other officials went to meet Sir Roger Cotam at 'the sign of the boore', suggesting an inn with a boar on its signage. As the boar had been Richard's personal badge, it seems unlikely that the mayor chose to meet Henry VII's representative beneath it by coincidence.

A year later, Henry VII visited York, and the city was at pains to put on a grand show for the new king. The city spent £66 putting on pageants to honour and acknowledge the victor of Bosworth. Pragmatism probably forced the city to set aside, at least publicly, its overt support for a deceased king who could no longer do them any more good. The reception Henry VII received was both splendid and deferent. However, the first Tudor king's problems with York were not over. Henry Percy, 4th Earl of Northumberland would be lynched by a mob at South Kilvington in Yorkshire during a tax riot, and rumour holds even today that it was vengeance for his suspected betrayal of Richard III at Bosworth. In 1491, another case was brought before the city officials when John Painter was accused of slandering the Earl of Northumberland 'saying he was a traitor who had betrayed king Richard'. Painter denied the charge and in turn accused Sir William Burton of calling Richard 'an ypocryte, a crochebake' and claiming that he had been 'beried in a dike like a dogge'. These charges were all denied, but demonstrate that Richard III's reputation still meant something in York.

Henry VII was forced to write to the mayor of York in 1494, warning that if he did not bring order to the city, 'I must and will put in other rulers that will rule and govern the city according to my laws'. For all its defiance and residual feelings for the old king, York also had to consider its own future, and it seems that the city officials decided that any resistance had to be limited to avoid comeback from the new king. That doesn't mean Richard isn't still remembered fondly in that region, though.

Little known fact:

During the Lambert Simnel Affair in 1487, when Henry VII faced the first attempt on his throne, York received particular attention from both sides. The rebels headed there, hoping for support, but York was reluctant to get involved. Henry repeatedly wrote to the city ordering it to remain vigilant against the threat of the invaders, mustering men there and placing the Earl of Northumberland in the city to ensure its cooperation.

Did Richard III Leave Evidence Of Where He Wanted To Be Buried?

Following the discovery of Richard III's remains beneath a car park in Leicester in 2012, a bitter debate erupted over the correct place for the bones to be permanently reinterred. The matter was in such dispute that

The statue of Richard III now located outside Leicester Cathedral. (Author's collection)

a group of Richard's collateral descendants brought a legal case to have the king reburied in York Minster rather than at Leicester Cathedral as was initially planned. Part of the argument relied on an assertion that Richard had left evidence of his intention to be buried at York which ought to be taken into consideration.

Objectively, several possible locations might have made a suitable burial place for Richard III, some more likely than others. Fotheringhay Castle was the traditional seat of the House of York. Richard's father had completed the establishment of a collegiate church at Saint Mary and All Saints Church in Fotheringhay, near to the castle. The second Duke of York, Edward, who had been killed at the Battle of Agincourt had requested that he be buried here and after his death in France, his bones were interred within the foundation he had begun, and his nephew had completed.

In 1476, Edward IV had ordered the transfer of the remains of his father, Richard, Duke of York and his brother Edmund, Earl of Rutland to Fotheringhay. Father and son had been killed at the Battle of Wakefield on 30 December 1460 and buried nearby, possibly at the Priory of St John the Evangelist near to the battlefield. For nine days between 21 July and 30 July, a funeral procession accompanied the exhumed bodies south to Fotheringhay with Richard acting as chief mourner for his father and brother. Two tombs flank the altar of St Mary and All Saints in Fotheringhay today, though these are later monuments erected on the instructions of Elizabeth I. The collegiate church in which the bodies were initially placed was destroyed during the Reformation. Shocked by the plight of her ancestors, Elizabeth ordered them moved into the main church. A tomb to the right of the altar commemorates Edward, 2nd Duke of York and to the left is a matching tomb for Richard's father Richard, Duke of York and his mother Cecily Neville, Duchess of York.

Fotheringhay might deserve consideration as a final resting place for Richard. It appears to have been intended as some sort of mausoleum for the House of York, and two former patriarchs had been laid to rest there along with one of Richard's older brothers. The suitability of Fotheringhay may have slipped once Edward IV became king and their house became the reigning royal family. A family mausoleum at the traditional seat of power was perfect for even the most senior noble family, but kings were a different matter altogether.

Most kings since the Conquest who were buried in England had been buried at Westminster Abbey. It had become the traditional place for monarchs to be laid to rest and so might be considered the natural choice for Richard III too. The burial of his wife Anne Neville within Westminster Abbey, near to the altar, might add weight to this supposition but is also a potential red herring. Richard might have intended to have created a tomb for both of them and have Anne transferred to join him after his own death, just as Henry VII would do with Elizabeth of York, but Richard also needed to think dynastically. He was negotiating a new marriage, the point of which must have been to try and father more sons. If he and his new wife had an heir who was to become king after him, then his dynastic credentials would rest with his second wife. It is far more likely that he would then plan to be buried with her, though this would not mean any disrespect to Anne, who was still buried in a place befitting a queen and a beloved wife.

Perhaps the most compelling argument can be made for an intention to be buried at St George's Chapel, Windsor. Edward IV had begun a Yorkist royal mausoleum there in which he himself was buried. In 1484, Richard III had ordered the transfer of Henry VI's remains from Chertsey Abbey to St George's and had them placed in a new tomb in one of the bays along the south aisle. It is possible that this was an act of atonement for his own, or at least his family's, part in Henry's death in 1471, though it may well have been to harness the growing cult springing up around Henry, who was starting to be seen as a potential saint. All of this recent focus makes St George's a strong candidate for the place Richard might have planned to be buried.

The claim that Richard may have intended to be buried in York is also feasible, at least until 1483. It was the premier city in the region he had, until then, lived most of his life within. Fotheringhay had become remote from him and Westminster and St George's were meant for kings, but why not York Minster for the north's most prominent lord? A belief that this intention continued is maintained by the establishment of a college of 100 priests at the Minster to pray for Richard and his family. This was still proceeding in March 1485, when Richard wrote about his concern that the priests should all be paid on time 'seeing that by their prayers we trust to be made more acceptable to god and his saints'. The establishment of a college does not necessarily equate with a planned mausoleum. Richard may well have intended to be buried in York during his time as Duke of Gloucester, but as king, it seems much less likely.

The dispute in this matter is moot anyway. Richard forfeited the right to choose where he lay when he lost the Battle of Bosworth, just as King John, Richard II and Henry VI had been denied their ideal resting place. Richard did not leave a will that remains or any other surviving document that can definitively state his intentions in this matter and perhaps could have influenced the reinternment, but ultimately, in 1485 at least, it would not have been up to Richard.

Little known fact:

Anne Neville's grave in Westminster Abbey is on the south side of the High Altar but remains unmarked. The simple burial might be a result of Richard's death later the same year and might even be a sign that he still planned to have her body transferred to join his. A brass plaque was placed on the wall close to the site of the grave in 1960. Part of the inscription reads 'In person she was seemly, amiable and beauteous ... And according to the interpretation of her name Anne full gracious.'

Glossary:

Collateral descendant is a legal term applied to the descendants of a person's brothers and sisters.

Why Did Shakespeare Write Richard III As Such A Villain?

For most people, the enduring image of King Richard III is Shakespeare's villain, who hobbles about the stage glorying in his own evil deeds, only to get his comeuppance at the Battle of Bosworth. The play is a masterpiece, an examination of the anti-hero and what drives men to dark deeds. It is a shame that, like so much of Shakespeare's dramatic fiction, it has become the accepted history of a man and his life. Much of Shakespeare's Richard III is pure myth, so how did the greatest writer in history select his greatest villain?

Most of the myths Shakespeare wrote about Richard III are easy to dismiss. We know he didn't have a limp or a withered arm and although he didn't have the kyphosis Shakespeare gave him, we now know he did have scoliosis. Those murders that Shakespeare accuses Richard of that cannot be dismissed out of hand are still so uncertain that Shakespeare cannot possibly have known the truth. His sources, such as Hall's Chronicle and Sir Thomas More, can be seen in his work but are themselves unreliable. Shakespeare rearranges geography so that Richard intercepts his nephew at Stony Stratford instead of Earl Rivers overshooting the meeting place. The gap in Shakespeare's Wars of the Roses plays between 1471 and 1483 means that the chronology is muddled and crammed together too.

The context in which Shakespeare wrote his play may prove a key to understanding why he selected Richard III as his villain and why he made him reveal his plotting to the audience throughout the play. *The Tragedy of King Richard the Third* was written in the early 1590's, probably around 1593. There had been religious upheavals throughout the century. It had been sixty years since Henry VIII's break with Rome after which his son had moved the country fully to the Protestant religion before Mary I changed the nation back to Catholicism and then Elizabeth I tried to implement a more tolerant form of Protestantism. The Spanish Armada had failed just five years earlier in 1588, attempting to drag England back into the Catholic fold again.

As Queen Elizabeth I reached sixty years of age, it was plain to all that she was not going to produce an heir of her body. Tension was mounting about the succession and Elizabeth herself was refusing to address the matter. As a difficult century of drastic and violent changes approached an end, another point of crisis was on the horizon. It has been suggested that Shakespeare remained a devout Catholic throughout his life and some of his most significant sponsors, such as the Earls of Essex and Southampton, were known Catholics. There is an interpretation of *Hamlet* as a call to arms for Catholics in England against Protestantism, and as Richard III hobbles onto the stage at the beginning of the play, it is entirely possible that an Elizabethan audience would have understood that they were looking at a very different person altogether.

Robert Cecil was the son of Elizabeth's most trusted advisor, William Cecil, Lord Burghley and he was being prepared to step into his father's shoes. In 1590 he had been appointed Secretary of State and along with his father was a firm Protestant. The father and son team were championing the succession of King James VI of Scotland to ensure England remained Protestant but Shakespeare's patrons, and perhaps Shakespeare himself, wanted a Catholic to take the throne after Elizabeth. Robert Cecil, as a matter of historical record, had kyphosis. He was, in Shakespeare's unpleasant parlance, 'a bunchback'. *Motley's History of the Netherlands* described Robert Cecil as a 'slight, crooked, hump-backed young gentleman, dwarfish in stature but with a face not irregular in feature, and thoughtful and subtle in expression'. The account went on to describe 'a disposition almost ingenuous, as compared to the massive dissimulation with which it was to be contrasted, and with what was, in aftertimes, to constitute a portion of his own character'. Doesn't that sound familiar?

King Richard III was perhaps an obvious candidate for the representation of evil. He had lost his life at the Battle of Bosworth a hundred years earlier to Elizabeth's grandfather. Elizabeth could count Edward IV and his children amongst her close family so any examination of the Wars of the Roses would need to carefully bear this in mind. Richard III had no one left to defend him or to be offended by the construction of an evil persona around him. The stories in circulation that Richard was, as Sir Thomas More termed it, a 'crookback', probably a lingering remembrance of his scoliosis, allowed Shakespeare to exaggerate him until he must have looked enough like Robert Cecil to enable contemporary audiences to understand what they were being asked to see. Taken out of context, it became a version of Richard III himself accepted as literal fact.

The character of Richard III is a villain who appeals to the audience. He jokes and charms his way through the play in a self-deprecating way that makes his outbursts of temper seem understandable. He tells the audience what he plans to do and challenges them to try and stop him, but the audience never does, instead finding themselves almost willing him to win. We almost like him, and we are meant to. Elizabeth I called Robert Cecil her 'little imp' and Shakespeare may have been pointing directly at Cecil's scheming for a Protestant, Scottish succession, which he was getting away with right under everyone's nose.

Richard III's story could also offer a lesson in the dangers of a contested succession. There had been serious problems after the death of Elizabeth's brother, Edward VI, but that was undoubtedly too close for comfort. The events of 1483 were remote enough that the story could offer a salutary lesson in the dangers of a disputed succession with people plotting for their own gain, just as Shakespeare might have been claiming Robert Cecil was. If this was what he meant his audiences to see, then Shakespeare made a lasting villain of King Richard III entirely by accident.

Little known fact:

Robert Cecil blamed his kyphosis on a nursemaid who he claimed dropped him as a small child. He went on to be promoted to Earl of Salisbury by James, who relied heavily on his talents.

Was Richard III A Good King?

The popular image of Richard III is that of a tyrant who snatched power, probably killed his nephews and got his comeuppance at the Battle of Bosworth. Many historians also subscribe to this view of Richard III, the most generous painting the events of 1483 as a panicked, unplanned response to a desperate and deteriorating situation whilst some adhere to the notion that he planned to take his nephew's throne all along. Either way, it is a usurpation for self-perseveration, and the killing of his nephews was a natural consequence. Those who believe Richard has been dealt a harsh hand by history take an opposing view; that taking the throne was done reluctantly as an act of duty, that he would never have even countenanced killing his brother's sons and that he was a good king. The two versions of Richard are entirely incompatible, so can we determine whether he was a 'good' king?

Medieval kings were expected to be many things and to fill many roles. Glory in war was desirable, but ultimately the defence of the realm from external attack and internal dissent was the key to a settled kingdom. Many in the fifteenth century and later clung to Henry V as an exemplar of the combination of the two. He was on such good terms with most of his nobility that the Southampton Plot was revealed to him by the man the plotters intended to replace Henry with. Renewing the war with France and the drastic success not only of Agincourt but subsequent campaigns that left Henry as legal heir to the throne of France at his untimely death was a good distraction from the internal problems his father had suffered but also attracted lasting and widespread fame.

As the medieval period progressed, a monarch was also expected to operate in conjunction with Parliament. Following Magna Carta, Henry III's reign had seen the growth of Parliament as a body that nominally advised the king but in practice also checked his worst tendencies. Usually, grants of taxation would only be made on the condition that the king rectified problems identified by Parliament and the increasingly self-confident body was not afraid to withhold money if the king failed to fall into line. By the Yorkist period, Parliament had secured for itself a role in judging and approving royal title to the crown. Richard, Duke of York had placed his claim before Parliament for their consideration, and both Edward IV and Richard III sought legitimacy through statute. As Parliament flexed its muscles, a good monarch would need to be able to work alongside the Lords and the Commons to achieve his aims.

Another role required of the monarch was that of a good lord to his nobles, in return for which he could expect their loyalty, even if he didn't always receive it. The monarch was responsible for keeping his nobles in check, ensuring that they didn't fall out spectacularly, as had happened during Henry VI's reign, and bringing them swiftly to terms if they did, or else punishing them suitably. For those further down the social ladder, the king was the ultimate arbiter of justice, and they would look to their monarch to ensure their lords were also restrained from abusing the rights of their tenants and servants. Essentially, the role of the monarch was to create balance in which all levels of society could feel safe and championed and in which justice was fair and accessible.

One of the main problems with judging Richard III against any of these measures is the brief time in which he attempted to establish himself on the throne before being removed and killed. During his time as Duke of Gloucester in the north of England, Richard had demonstrated a commitment to good lordship and to fair justice that meant he was widely respected and there is little to suggest he would not have planned to translate this reputation to the national stage. The only Parliament that sat during Richard's reign in 1484 appears to have included many measures aimed at improving access to justice for the common man, improving trade for English merchants and providing some degree of conciliation with traditional enemies in his failure to attaint Lady Margaret Beaufort in particular. However, the fact that there had been a rebellion within four months of his accession points to deeper problems that had to be addressed.

Richard's apparent concern for the common man and for equitable justice was at odds with the prejudices and interests of the majority of the nobility. The nobility had a vested interest in the long-standing status quo that Richard appears to have been keen to reform. For a monarch, reconciling his senior nobles to his policy aims was a crucial factor in delivering successful government, and in this, Richard conspicuously failed. The Howard family were to be the only dukes or earls to fight for Richard at Bosworth, and that exposes an insurmountable failure in his attempts to be accepted as a ruler.

Perhaps the most important role for a monarch was securing their dynasty and passing the crown on to an heir, preferably to their own oldest surviving son. For Richard, personal tragedy in the loss of his son and then his wife in quick succession also meant dynastic disaster. The problem was not insurmountable if he were to remarry quickly and father another son to follow him, but Richard was denied time to complete this most important of tasks. In a dynastic sense too, Richard failed to meet the criteria of a 'good' king. His reign would mark the end of a Plantagenet dynasty that had ruled England since 1154 and that loss is almost the worst stain possible on a monarch's record.

There is evidence to suggest that, given time, Richard III could have been remembered as a good king. If he had been on the throne for longer and the fate of his nephews had become more clear, his reforms to justice had taken hold, and he had been able to bring the nobility more tightly into the fold, his rule might have been remembered as in the public good. He was interested in aggression on the continent and even talked of crusades, but internal problems prevented him from looking outside his own borders. Luck appears to have been on Richard's side in October 1483, but by August 1485, even this had deserted him. Perhaps most of all, for failing to secure his dynasty and allowing the crown to slip not only from the heads of the House of York but also the Plantagenet ruling dynasty that had lasted 331 years, and despite glimpses of promise, Richard III cannot be considered to have been a good king.

Little known fact:

Henry VIII seems to have greatly admired Henry V and tried to emulate his achievements, invading France early in his reign and even executing Yorkist noble Edmund de la Pole just before he departed in 1513, just as Henry V had executed members of the Southampton Plot just before leaving for France in 1415.

Can You Tell From Richard's Portrait He Was A Good Man?

The Daughter of Time by Josephine Tey is a 1951 detective novel that for many remains their first introduction to a more sympathetic view of Richard III. The premise of the story is that while Detective Alan Grant is injured and recovering in hospital, he is left staring at a portrait of Richard III and decides to use his enforced rest to investigate the crimes this man is accused of. What initially strikes Detective Grant is that in his opinion, the face in the portrait does not match the historical figure he has heard such terrible things about. In essence, his detective's instinct tells him this is not the face of a criminal. Despite being a work of fiction, *The Daughter of Time* has influenced a great many people, but can a portrait really tell us what Richard was like?

There are three surviving early portraits of Richard III, though none are from within his lifetime. Some later images seem to be based on, and were most likely traced from, a portrait in the Royal Collection. This image has been dated from around 1504–1520 and is believed to be based on a lost original of an image from Richard's lifetime. The Royal Collection portrait shows Richard in a sumptuous black velvet gown trimmed with fur against a deep red background. Richard has a large and expensively jewelled collar around his neck and a similarly impressive brooch on his hat. He wears rings on his right hand on the thumb, his third finger and his little finger, which he is either removing a ring from or placing a ring onto. Richard's face shows a stern expression, but x-ray examination has revealed that the facial features have been altered to accentuate the thin lips and narrow-eyed glare. The alterations appear to have been made at the time of painting or very shortly afterwards, suggesting that the artist first copied the lost original and then changed it, possibly at the instruction of another, to give a more sinister appearance. It is also clear

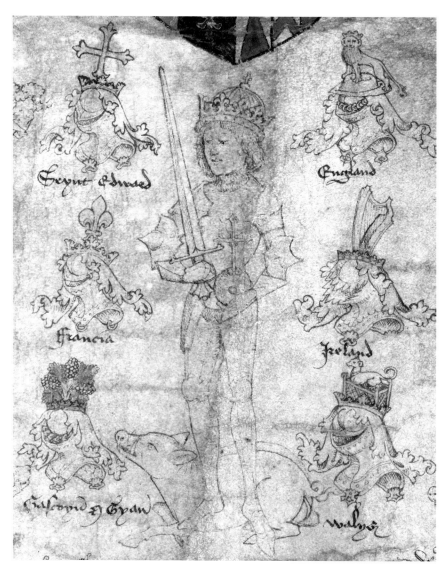

The depiction of Richard III from the Rous Roll, by Warwickshire antiquary John Rous. Rous praised Richard during his lifetime but shortly after his death described him as the Antichrist.

that the right shoulder has been similarly overpainted to raise it above the level of the left. Richard's skeleton has revealed that scoliosis meant this element of his appearance was, to some degree, accurate but must have been passed over in the original, showing that it was not something Richard would accept being publicised. This portrait provided the basis for fashionable copies decades later, each with changes, but all showing the pinched, cruel features.

A second early portrait of Richard believed to date from between 1523 and 1555 is rarely used as a depiction of the king. Amongst those held by the Society of Antiquities, it is dark, perhaps needing restoration, and it shows Richard holding a broken sword upright, suggesting the breaking of his kingship. Richard's left hand is clearly deformed, possibly following Sir Thomas More's version of a withered arm, and in this image, the left shoulder is significantly higher than the right. Examinations of this painting have shown that the left shoulder was in fact much higher in the original but has been reduced at some point. This portrait also seems to show the softest representation of Richard's facial features, with fuller lips and a less focused glare.

A second portrait within the collection of the Society of Antiquaries is equally fascinating. It is believed to date from a similar time to the painting in the Royal Collection so may well have also been a copy taken from a now lost original painted during Richard's lifetime. Cleaning of this portrait in 2007 appears to reveal the method used to make Richard's appearance fit a sinister narrative he undoubtedly would have avoided in images created during his own lifetime. Although the eyes in this portrait do not share the same narrowed glare of others, the restoration showed that the mouth had been moved up from the original position to create a more severe expression. Revealed in its original location, the portrait is made slightly softer, though it remains one of a serious, stern man. In this picture, Richard is either removing or putting on a ring on his wedding finger, leading to suggestions that this portrait may have been copied from one created in early 1485 as part of marriage negotiations with Spain and Portugal after the death of Anne Neville, showing Richard ready to consider marriage again. In this portrait, Richard's left shoulder appears raised above the right. It is possible that the switching of hands with rings and the changing side of the raised shoulders was a result of the original being traced so that it could be painted facing left or right depending on the intended use and positioning of the portrait. If the artist failed to alter the side with the raised shoulder or the hand with rings on and instead simply copied the reversed tracing, the rings and raised shoulder could easily switch sides.

There are a number of issues with the study of the available portraiture of King Richard III. The facial reconstruction completed after the discovery of his skeleton does not entirely solve these problems because it relies on guesswork to apply skin thickness and the like. The first issue is that none of the surviving early portraits date from within Richard's lifetime. The second is the degree of alteration visible within the paintings. It was previously thought that the additions and exaggerations of a raised shoulder were mere Tudor propaganda, but it is now clear that it was actually the representation of something Richard himself would have wanted to be hidden in portraiture. This makes the assessment of the changes to facial expression more difficult to pick apart.

It might be relevant to consider the purpose of any portrait, contemporary or later. In an age before photography or high levels of connection and communication, a portrait was meant to tell a story even more than to provide a likeness. This is nowhere more visible than in the paintings of Elizabeth I during her later years. Portraits commissioned by Richard would have sought to flatter and serve a purpose. He would not wish his raised shoulder visible in an age that too often associated physical conditions with a corruption of the soul. Richard set out to distinguish his reign from that of his brother Edward IV, whose portrait at the Society of Antiquaries is notably round-faced and soft and this might have been a deliberate step either in Richard's lifetime or afterwards when these portraits tried to tell a story of a king. Edward IV's reputation was as a larger than life, womanising glutton in his later years and Richard's was as a scheming tyrant. Fashionable patrons seeking fashionable artwork would want to demonstrate their understanding of the rulers who had gone before and each picture would have been required to tell a story. In *A Daughter of Time*, it is the beginning of Alan Grant's journey, and these portraits can offer the same launchpad, but they can never tell us the whole story.

Little known fact:

A number of the surviving images of Richard III and other monarchs date from the late Elizabethan and early Stuart period when it became fashionable to display sets of portraits of former rulers. Most decorated the long galleries of great houses and owning a full set became a way to show off. In many cases, these were painted directly onto panels that lined the wall rather than being individually hung paintings.

Conclusion

In the case of King Richard III, separating fact from fiction presents challenges only a handful of other historical figures share. The popular image of Richard has been shaped almost entirely by a work of fiction that leaves him with few, if any, redeeming features and which for many will represent their first and only impression of him. Shakespeare's play in undoubtedly a masterpiece but the greatest tragedy is that for so long, it has been accepted as history rather than drama. Having said that, the play and the controversy it can spark may lie at the heart of the reason Richard III has enjoyed such a high profile for centuries despite only two years on the throne.

Some of the myths that cling to Richard III can be quickly dispelled. Shakespeare's representation of him killing the Duke of Somerset at the First Battle of St Albans when Richard would have been two years old is nonsensical, except that it serves the conflated timeline Shakespeare was forced to employ and some foreshadowing. It might also represent the execution of a different Duke of Somerset after the Battle of Tewkesbury in 1471. Other aspects of Shakespeare's character are exaggerations of the truth. Richard had scoliosis but not kyphosis, and he did not have a limp or a withered arm. It is likely that these were intended as outward markers of Richard's corrupted soul, a favourite trope in previous centuries.

The problem with sifting through many of the stories that surround Richard III is the lack of decisive evidence one way or the other. His involvement in the death of Henry VI was rumoured at the time and in later accounts, yet there is no real proof he was, or was not, involved. A view of Richard harbouring a long-term desire to snatch his brother's throne seems deeply unlikely and is contradicted by much of the evidence of a decade or more of good and loyal service. Few can have expected Edward IV to die so early and so Richard's prospects of putting any plan into action must have been so remote as to seem impossible, yet he made no suspicious move at all.

A difficult and traumatic childhood saw Richard losing close family members, including his father and one older brother whilst he was just eight years old. He was abandoned at Ludlow to face a hostile army and trusted to the leniency of a king his father was at war with and experiences such as this must have left a mark on a growing boy. A spell in exile that was revolutionised by his brother's seizure of the crown must have demonstrated how precarious life could be, how quickly things could change and how taking control of a situation could be the best route to solving problems. There is evidence that Richard provided a level of 'good lordship' during his time in the north that created a lingering well of affection for him. His influence was used to improve the region's financial situation, and he seems to have been committed to the improvement of justice for the common man, unafraid to push against the vested interests of more powerful factions because of his close relationship to the king.

The evidence provides a picture of Richard that is not all good. He was cruel to the elderly Countess of Oxford and was part of the process that saw his mother-in-law the Countess of Warwick declared legally dead so that her lands and titles could be divided between Richard and George. There is little doubt that Richard was willing to be ruthless in the pursuit and protection of what he believed was his. Edward IV had granted him the Oxford lands and overseen the partition of the Warwick patrimony, so Richard was not the final arbiter of these dealings, but he was prepared to benefit from them. It is questionable whether these incidents particularly mark Richard out from his peers. Throughout the medieval period and perhaps particularly during the upheavals and reversals of the Wars of the Roses, any magnate had to work and fight to maintain what they held.

As king, there are glimpses of the promise of greatness, but it was not realised. Richard's Parliament demonstrated a reforming impetus that appears to carry on from his own attitudes during his time in the north, but as a singular occurrence, its importance is as easy to overstate as it is to dismiss. Luck appeared to be on Richard's side in October 1483, but a rebellion so early in his reign is a signal that all was not well. The identification of the October revolt as Buckingham's Rebellion is a misnomer that probably covers up the real purpose of an uprising in favour of a Tudor claimant of the Lancastrian line in exile on the continent. Personal and dynastic tragedy followed, and Richard's plans to remarry in particular seem to attract controversy. The evidence shows he was negotiating for a match with a Portuguese princess, yet the story of his intention to marry his own niece lingers about him as a sinister stain on his character.

By 1485, the lack of support available to Richard at Bosworth demonstrates that he had been unable to translate the fierce loyalty he seems to have inspired in those close to him over the years onto the national stage. His willingness to challenge vested interests, which might have seemed odd but been tolerated in the north, became a serious threat in a king and alienated those whose support Richard needed to win. A personal feud with the Stanley family dating back to Hornby in 1469 might ultimately have cost Richard his crown and his life.

It is the events of 1483 that have long overshadowed Richard's reputation and will continue to until more unambiguous evidence comes to light. The manner in which he took the throne cannot clearly be confirmed; was he plotting it for years? Did he react in panic to the problems he found in London in May? Did he genuinely feel that becoming king was his duty after the revelations about his brother's marriage? The same events and the same evidence can be viewed by two different people, and diametrically opposed conclusions can be reached and reasonably argued. The murder of the Princes in the Tower is the epitome of these problems. There is no evidence beyond their disappearance that Richard murdered them, or that they were murdered at all. There is as much evidence and likelihood that they were killed by another or that they did not die at all, yet for many, Richard remains convicted in the court of public opinion. The purpose of this book has been to try and separate fact from fiction wherever possible and in those less clear cases, to provide the reader with as much information as can be offered to help decide his guilt or innocence.

The Richard III of fiction is evident in Shakespeare's work, where he is the scheming arch-criminal, but it is clear in other more recent works of fiction in which he is painted as a hero with barely a fault in his personality. The Richard of fact is somewhere to be found in between these Hollywood extremities but seems likely to remain hotly debated for the foreseeable future. He was a real person, the same as you and I. He had experiences that shaped him, dreams that inspired him and fears that drove him. More than anything else, it is a fact that King Richard III was a man of his times and should be judged as such.